Delivering Bad News in Good Ways:

Turn difficult conversations into purposeful dialogue, positive outcomes, & focused results in 3 easy steps

Alison H.Sigmon, M.Ed., PMP

Includes bibliographical references.

ISBN-13: 978-0692701706
ISBN-10: 0692701702

1. Business-Communication. 2. Psychology, Interpersonal Skills.

DEDICATION

This book is dedicated to all the people with whom I've had the pleasure to work or train over the years. Thank you for being the teacher to this student.

CONTENTS

Dedication   3

Introduction: Delivering Bad News in Good Ways
Better way to prepare and communicate bad news   5

Chapter 1: No Innocent Parties
Take initiative to step up or risk the project
driving off a cliff   12

Chapter 2: Lure of Magical Thinking
Short-term gains, long-term loss - the impact
of delaying the inevitable   20

Chapter 3: Why Is It So Tough to Deliver Bad News?
Oh, the places we go with our stories (fears)   33

Chapter 4: Welcome to the SED Method
Overview of the SED tool for delivery:
Separate, Evaluate, & Deliver   55

Chapter 5: Separate Step of the SED Method
Get the facts straight first   69

Chapter 6: Evaluate Step of the SED Method
Connecting the dots   113

Chapter 7: Deliver Step of the SED Method
Craft the statement with an eye to the receiver   139

Chapter 8: After SED - Now What?
Let's talk it out   156

Chapter 9: The End & the Beginning
Looking back to move forward   174

Acknowledgments   180

Bibliography & Credits   184

About the Author   188

Let's Connect!   189

INTRODUCTION:

DELIVERING BAD NEWS IN GOOD WAYS

BETTER WAY TO PREPARE AND COMMUNICATE BAD NEWS

LET THE BAND AID RIP!

"Listen, I've got information that is important to share…if you don't want to hear it other people do. So let's quiet down."

Amid boos, curses, and protests that rippled through the crowd, this is what the executive said in a mobile phone-made video published on *YouTube* on February 10, 2016. In it employees at Carrier Corporation, a subsidiary of United Technologies, assembled to hear for the first time an announcement that would forever change the lives of 1,400 employees and their families.

About 10 seconds into the video, the executive, seen faintly in the distance, said, *"It became clear the best way to stay competitive and protect the business for long term is to move production from our facility in Indianapolis to Monterrey, Mexico…"*

In addition to the announcement about relocating the production facility, the executive noted plans to move the distribution center as well. Feeling pressure for higher investment returns, United Technologies reportedly is looking to cut costs wherever it can in an effort to stay competitive.

The executive continues, saying, *"I want to be clear. This is strictly a business decision."* More disgruntled words of protest erupt. The crowd's anxiousness and frustration grow as movement around the hall increases.

I read about this in Nelson Schwartz's *NY Times* article titled *Carrier Workers See Costs, Not Benefits, of Global Trade.* While the focus of the article was about the global trade debate currently raging in the United States, I was struck by the approach executive management took with delivering this clearly bad – no, devastating – news.

Management chose to take the "rip the Band Aid off" approach, but based on the reaction of the employees, this was exactly how NOT to deliver bad news.

The executive assured the crowd that the move was not a reflection of their work and that relocation would have no immediate impact on their jobs, but the employees likely did not hear any of that part.

| 6 |

Delivering Bad News in Good Ways:
Turn difficult conversations into purposeful dialogue, positive outcomes, & focused results in 3 easy steps

Why? Because of the shock they felt hearing it for the first time. The emotional impact was so great it was likely equal to hearing for the first time about the death of a loved one. Nothing else can be processed inside that moment.

Deeper in the video we learn management made the announcement before working with union representatives. Mr. Schwartz also confirmed via email with me that the employees had no advance knowledge of the company's intention prior to this announcement.

So while it appears little advanced groundwork was done to ease employees into the new future of the company, the executive continues with the following:

"We still have a job to do. We have to take care of what needs to be done every day and continue to do it well just like we do…We are committed to treating you with respect throughout this transition."

It seems respect would include consideration for how the bad news was delivered. While debate lingers in the business world about how best to deliver bad news to employees, with the "rip the Band Aid off" approach among the methods recommended, there seems to be some room to consider a more empathic approach than what the Carrier executives chose. Consider the following:

▶ How could Carrier management done this differently?

▶ Where did the delivery of the bad news fall down?

▶ What could the leadership have done in advance of the announcement to mitigate the response?

The structure of the executive's news was acceptable, but the delivery stumbled. It was received as insensitive, inconsiderate, and one-sided. Basically, employees had no voice at the decision-making table. It is tough to get buy-in that way, and for Carrier the result ended up being a public relations nightmare across media and political platforms.

This is what we will address in this book. While the "rip the Band Aid" approach might be the right thing in some cases, there are actions we can take in advance to have what economists call a "soft landing" when delivering bad news.

Delivering Bad News in Good Ways:
Turn difficult conversations into purposeful dialogue, positive outcomes, & focused results in 3 easy steps

| 7 |

SO HERE WE GO

Having spent many years working with startups to launch, grow, and raise funds for digital and ecommerce businesses, to create and deliver training programs for Fortune 1000 companies, and to consult in project management for government and corporations around the world, I have experienced plenty of situations to mine for topics for this book.

In addition to my work in business, I also have a graduate degree in psychology/clinical counseling and was a therapist for a number of years. Prior to that I was in the active duty and reserve US Air Force for more that 12 years. That experience coupled with my business and counseling experiences gave me a unique insight into communication, community systems, teamwork, management, and leadership.

Rare is the project that runs smoothly. In addition, the ever-evolving digital era continues to change the way we work. This new environment is fast and furious, and project challenges are a way of life.

When I first started in project management, the focus was on the technical side. I understood the reason for this, but it was not always where I hit the speed bumps with my projects, and I bet it is not where you normally run into trouble, either.

COMMON DENOMINATOR

Managers are needed for a variety of project types. Some are small and others are large and complex. The golden rule in managing projects is not to overdo. In other words, make the plan.appropriate to the size and complexity of the project and only use what you really need to get the project done.

It is normal to use different tools and to trim steps to accommodate that rule. That is part of the art of managing projects and work. While the project process and tools may change from project to project, one common denominator runs throughout any project: *People.*

Welcome to my speed bump and apparently the speed bump of the thousands I have either had the pleasure to train, coach, or work with on projects.

| 8 |

Delivering Bad News in Good Ways:
Turn difficult conversations into purposeful dialogue, positive outcomes, & focused results in 3 easy steps

When it comes to people, we know one size does not fit all. A smart project manager or supervisor regularly checks their ego at the door. They also make adjustments in personal style to accommodate the style of the person with whom they are working. This is particularly important when it comes to delivering bad news.

HOW THIS BOOK WORKS

This book is intended to be a quick read and an easy, hands-on reference guide with supplemental information you can access at my website www.alisonsigmon.com.

It provides a process for delivering bad news, called the **SED Method,** which stands for Separate, Evaluate, and Deliver. Using acronyms is common in business books. Although it might seem overused, let's play to our strengths.

Acronyms offer easy-to-remember techniques needed particularly in stressful situations, such as letting someone know a critical deadline is going to be missed, a person is not meeting performance expectations, or 30 percent of project funding has been wiped from the budget but the deadline remains the same.

We kick off each chapter with a contextual story to help guide the experience. As we move through the SED Method process explanation, we serve up research, tips, and story vignettes in addition to the lead story for each chapter to create bridges between the steps and your experience.

The book also provides links to worksheets so you can practice and apply the techniques. Tips and FAQs are also included here and at http://alisonsigmon. com/worksheets.

IS THIS BOOK FOR ME?

Delivering bad news is rarely at the top of a person's list of things they can't wait to do. Consider the following questions:

▶ **Why** is delivering bad news so hard to do?

▶ **What** are the tactics we use to avoid or postpone it?

Delivering Bad News in Good Ways:
Turn difficult conversations into purposeful dialogue, positive outcomes, & focused results in 3 easy steps

| 9 |

- ▸ **How** do we make it worse by putting it off?

- ▸ What can we do to **get out of our own way** when faced with the need to deliver bad news?

- ▸ Is there a **process** for delivering bad news in good ways?

We could go deep with each of these questions. The field of psychology has tackled many of them. The irony is it often comes down to individual perspective and the stories we tell ourselves.

We will take a look at what is behind delaying the delivery of bad news, but only as it applies to helping you assess *your* style, so you can be conscious of when you use tactics that hold you back. Once you have awareness of what gets in your way, you have a better shot at not procrastinating, avoiding, or overreacting.

You will also learn how to assess others so you can prepare the delivery of bad news in a way that best suits the receiver. Often at such times we're so focused on getting the content right that we stumble with the delivery.

This book is not for you if you have no trouble delivering bad news. Hats off to you if that is the case. We want to know the secret of your success! If you care to share, I would love to hear your thoughts and stories at my website at www.alisonsigmon.com or drop me a line at alison@alisonsigmon.com.

This book is for you if you find yourself procrastinating, withholding, self-abasing, avoiding, ignoring, rationalizing, or martyring (no, you did not read that last word incorrectly) in the face of delivering news you think will hurt, damage, or somehow negatively impact the other person, people, or yourself.

WHAT YOU GET FOR YOUR TIME

In the spirit of Socratic questions, you will get the so, so what, and so now what of communicating bad news in exchange for the time you invest in this book.

You will have the opportunity to learn a process to prepare and deliver bad news to someone in a positive way for a more productive, dialogue-driven, solutions-oriented outcome.

It provides anecdotes, research-supported facts, and "in the field" tips for separating fact from opinion, emotion from thought, and reality from stories (we tell ourselves).

BASICALLY, THE PROCESS HELPS US GET OUT OF OUR OWN WAY.

Along with the facts that you may or may not want to show off to your colleagues and friends, I hope you have moments that make you smile, laugh, reflect, and feel confident in future challenging exchanges.

You will have an opportunity to recognize your own communication preferences and those of others, which will get you more than halfway there with delivering bad news (or what YOU think is bad news - more about that later!).

While this book focuses on delivering bad news on projects, it is not limited to that use. The best processes move beyond singular application.

A solid process can be modified and adapted so it can be used in most any situation. This saves time and energy because it gives you a basic framework as a foundation that can then be adjusted based on the current state.

So, let's get started!

Delivering Bad News in Good Ways:
Turn difficult conversations into purposeful dialogue, positive outcomes, & focused results in 3 easy steps

| 11 |

CHAPTER 1:

NO INNOCENT PARTIES

TAKE INITIATIVE TO STEP UP OR RISK THE PROJECT DRIVING OFF A CLIFF

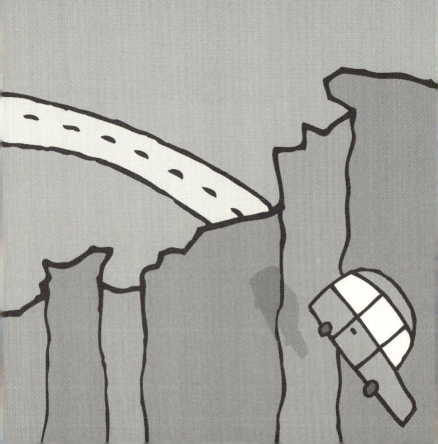

"ROCK STAR" FLAMES OUT

Executives at one of the nation's oldest and most respected healthcare companies had begun whispering their concerns to each other. Quarter over quarter, the company's market share was steadily declining. The stalwart firm, with decades of exemplary service to customers, employees, and communities across the country, was treading water in the age of digital growth.

Employees discussed the state of the company in hushed tones; talking aloud about such things simply was not done. Their confidence in the company's ability to bounce back was starting to waver.

With the company's future hanging in the balance, executives went looking for a "rock star" that could pull their most profitable division into the 21st century with an innovative digital project expected to leave the competition in the dust.

With the solution identified, the team in place, and budget approved, all that was left was to get the project manager in place. Based on the present situation, the leadership believed the person had to come from outside the company. The executives wanted new blood for their new and improved future.

Finding the rock star wasn't hard. Jon, a charismatic, fast-talking business development specialist was a highly sought-after, high profile hire with a seeming Midas touch. As far as the executives could see, Jon, who worked at a competing healthcare company, had a solid track record. With deep experience in sales and the added benefit of an advanced medical degree, Jon knew the ropes and never failed to deliver results, even in the "eleventh hour."

After a negotiation ending with several sweeteners to Jon's contract and unanimous agreement that his lack of digital experience would not be an issue, the executives congratulated themselves on landing such a big fish. But if they had looked more closely, they would have questioned Jon's methods and avoided an expensive, embarrassing mess.

Whispers took off throughout the company like tendrils on a thick vine. The buzz was palpable. Not only would this industry rock star recast the old company from bleak to unique, it would raise the company's profile (and

Delivering Bad News in Good Ways:
Turn difficult conversations into purposeful dialogue, positive outcomes, & focused results in 3 easy steps

| 13 |

value estimates!) among the hip and trendy with its hot, groundbreaking digital transformation.

The team, assigned before Jon was hired to lead the multi-million dollar project, was made up of highly experienced people eager to work on what the company grapevine now called the "Savior Project." It was all smiles when Jon was introduced to his team. With the halo effect in full force, the team had total confidence he'd save the day while catapulting their careers in the process. Their smiles beamed; he beamed back.

Jon knew he had a steep ramp with the "Savior Project" so, true to form, he dove deep into the division's content, products, and resources, and he amassed understanding of the latest trends in the industry. He conducted interviews, read extensively, and blazed through training on digital products and performance.

The first few months were exactly what everyone expected – the project's performance was organized, clear, and well documented. Jon had talent and skill and did not delay using experiences from past projects to get this one going. They had served him well in the past so, of course, it would be the same this time, or so he thought. Confidence was never an issue for Jon.

Over the ensuing months, mild confusion started settling in among the team.

The tasks delegated to team members at the beginning of the week typically changed by the end of the week. Jon, moving fast but still feeling the strain to produce early and often, adjusted the team's work priorities constantly, sometimes after nothing more than an off-hand comment by an executive or internal customer.

The team never seemed to finish anything. Frustration mounted. It got to the point that it seemed the only time the team felt productive was when Jon was off networking with vendors, customers, and execs, only to have that work undone upon his return.

Jon, feeling the pressure for results multiplying, reacted with even more changes of direction. He managed executive opinion by cloaking the absence of results in his "fail fast, learn fast" approach. Still dazzled by him, the executives left him alone.

| 14 |

Delivering Bad News in Good Ways:
Turn difficult conversations into purposeful dialogue, positive outcomes, & focused results in 3 easy steps

Back with the team, chaos grew like a virus as Jon implemented whatever new concepts he had learned or recommendations he had received from his network. This went on for more than a year.

When executives finally realized the depth of the problem, the $2.3 million project had blown past $13.1 million with no hope of completion in sight.

Jon was removed from the project, which was canceled quickly. People again spoke in hushed tones as they wondered what happened. A team member fed up with the charade finally spoke up.

> *"He knew it was bad for a long time, but he wouldn't get out of his own way. His ego couldn't suffer failure and he wouldn't ask for help. Ironic, because he got failure anyway — we all did."*

The outspoken team member, like all the team members, knew the problem. Not asking for help early on sealed Jon's fate — and the fate of the project. But the question lingers — Why?

The easy answer is to chuck Jon into the egomaniac bin and be done with it, but it is not that simple.

Personality aside, Jon had a proven track record for getting results. What he lacked in subject matter expertise for this specific project he could make up by listening to the experts around him while using his management skills to guide and steer the project.

Jon was not a bad person — he just got in his own way. And as we will see in the next section, he was not the only one to have this issue on the project.

Delivering Bad News in Good Ways:
Turn difficult conversations into purposeful dialogue, positive outcomes, & focused results in 3 easy steps

| 15 |

COMMUNICATION 101

Lots of Monday morning quarterbacking uncovered layers of issues that made it clear Jon's project failed for a variety of reasons, the greatest of which is that no one communicated effectively or bothered to deliver the bad news about the state of the project until it was too late.

In my experience, communication is the exchange of information between individuals or groups using a medium most appropriate to the depth and sensitivity of the subject matter, culture, and people involved. Basically, use the right tool with the right person at the right time.

There is a trail of evidence suggesting no single person was at fault. The failure to speak up sooner about the state of the project started before Jon was even hired. As it turns out, communication of bad news was avoided at multiple turns at the onset.

Let's follow the breakdown of communication in this situation.

SHARED RESPONSIBILITY

▶ COMPANY CULTURE

The company culture had an unstated but obviously understood rule that discouraged outward communication about negatives associated with the business.

The "whispers of worries" and "hushed tones" suggest this and provide the first signs of trouble ahead. We can confidently infer that bad news was poorly tolerated and avoided at just about any cost.

▶ THE LEADERSHIP

The executives who hired Jon do not get away without some responsibility. They knew their "savior," hand-picked for a digital project, had no digital experience. Yet during the year he worked on the project, they never asked for proof of progress. Their "magical thinking," something we will cover in Chapter 2, led to an absence of regular reality checks through the lifecycle of the project.

| 16 |

Delivering Bad News in Good Ways:
Turn difficult conversations into purposeful dialogue, positive outcomes, & focused results in 3 easy steps

This suggests the leadership was far too invested in its decision not to challenge each other or challenge Jon's lack of action – even when mounting evidence suggested otherwise. We see this when the story notes that the leadership was "still dazzled" by him. We will explore more about this in Chapter 4.

This led to inflating the budget to $13.1 million before canceling the project. We should not be surprised, really, considering the hero/scapegoat culture Jon's story implies. This is something else we will cover in Chapter 4 – when emotional investment in an outcome leads to bias and flawed thinking. This impacts communication of all types to include delivering bad news.

Basically, leadership was culpable in the failure to deliver bad news about the status of the company and with Jon in a timely manner. Their avoidance was fueled by rationalizations. In Chapter 3 we will get into what that is, how it happens, and what you can do in response.

▶ THE TEAM

You could argue that everyone involved, even the members of Jon's team, ignored all the red flags along the way. And you would be right.

Affected by culture and leadership, members of the team likely did not feel they could 1) engage and challenge Jon directly about his methods or 2) up-channel the issues to leadership if Jon did not respond to the team. In Chapter 7 we will consider what the team could have done to deliver the bad news with confidence in ways that Jon and the leadership could hear.

Let's not forget that the team was also starry-eyed about Jon and the "Savior Project." Their behavior suggests a deep emotional investment in the project's success, which likely prevented them from speaking up sooner. We will consider the impact of this in Chapter 4.

When the story notes that "The team never seemed to finish anything. Frustration mounted," it suggests the they felt discontented and demoralized, and yet did not speak up even when members knew it was off the rails with little hope for improvement.

Delivering Bad News in Good Ways:
Turn difficult conversations into purposeful dialogue, positive outcomes, & focused results in 3 easy steps

| 17

By the end of the project, a pattern of behavior had set in. The only way to break a pattern is to interrupt it, but that did not happen until it was far too late. Chapter 6 offers some perspective on this as you will see.

Eventually a team member who was fed up delivered the bad news, but not until the project had been canceled. This fact reinforces the company culture of avoiding disclosure of bad news. An environment like this is often a breeding ground for passive-aggressive behavior. We will explore more about that as a defense mechanism in Chapter 3.

▶ JON

There is no doubt that Jon has a big share of responsibility in the failure of this project. Jon bought into his myth. It is tempting to make a beeline toward blaming ego, but it is more complicated, and the evidence does not completely support it.

Skills. Jon's reputation suggests he likely had never dealt with the level of issues associated with this project. Reflective people learn from failure, but Jon's story suggests he never had faced this kind of situation. As a result, he did not seem to have the skills to manage it. But by the end of this book you will.

Expertise. Jon's success was in business development. Digital was completely new to him. As a result, he was constantly behind on the learning curve. This led him to get stuck in the fact-gathering stage, which is something we will consider in Chapter 5 when we review "objective questions."

Method. It is said we need the right tool for the right job. While Jon possessed tried-and-true methods, he struggled with adapting them effectively because he was constantly riding the learning curve. We will consider what this means in Chapter 4 and Chapter 8.

Self-awareness. Jon was well aware of his strengths, but woefully unaware of his weaknesses. Self-awareness, which we will consider in Chapter 6, is a critical component of leadership and management of projects and teams. If you are not aware of your blind spots, then you will most likely be blindsided by them at regular intervals.

| 18 |

Delivering Bad News in Good Ways:
Turn difficult conversations into purposeful dialogue, positive outcomes, & focused results in 3 easy steps

DON'T BE A JON

By the end of this book you will have a simple three-step process for delivering bad news in good ways in a timely manner. You will also gain an advantage Jon did not have – a better understanding of how to get out of your own way in the process.

Out of his element and afraid of failing, Jon felt stuck about where or how to begin what had become an overwhelming task.

When we feel our skill level does not match the job in front of us, we feel challenged. As we move through this book, we will visit the how and why of this and what we can do in response.

Jon believed the "where" and "how" would come to him eventually. As we saw from his story, Jon was wrong. But what drove this way of thinking?

As we will see in Chapter 2, it is very human to delay or avoid doing something we think is difficult, even when we know doing it is best for all involved.

CHAPTER TAKEAWAYS

▶ Communication defined

▶ Communication breakdown responsibility

▶ Why we remain silent: Fear, ego, lack of skills, rationalization

▶ Faulty and absent communication has no innocent parties

CHAPTER 2:

LURE OF MAGICAL THINKING

SHORT-TERM GAINS, LONG-TERM LOSS - THE IMPACT OF DELAYING THE INEVITABLE

WHEN THE MAGIC OF THE MIND GOES WRONG

Nancy spent the better half of her adult life as a business owner. Her businesses ran the gamut, from day care centers to private investigation. It was the private investigation work that landed her in the then-profitable field of subrogation.

Subrogation is the right of an insurer to pursue a third party who causes a loss to the insured. Often it involves two insurance companies going back and forth behind the scenes to verify the events and amounts paid.

Nancy loved the work and excelled at it. As her client list grew, so did her bank account. Her reputation preceded her in many network circles, and her business was a hot commodity.

For several years, her subrogation work made her the go-between in her state for insurance companies, which yielded them sizable returns. One former CFO of a major nationwide insurance company said he was impressed with her firm's work because, before her involvement, up to 30 percent of the subrogation effort in their company had to be written off.

Then, Nancy received a piece of news that rocked her world — and not in a good way. The state in which she operated was considering changing the rules to limit subrogation work to attorneys and people trained in the legal field.

It was rumored that if the change went into effect, insurance companies would likely bring all subrogation work in-house instead of outsourcing, as many were doing at the time. Nancy, a contractor, was not an attorney and did not have formal legal training.

At first, she reacted casually and seemed unconcerned. When asked, she insisted there was no cause for worry. She believed people like her would be protected.

"They would be foolish to do this. We recover far too much money for insurance companies. This will never be enacted…it's impossible. We'll be fine," she said repeatedly and confidently. She carried on like usual and said nothing to her team.

Delivering Bad News in Good Ways:
Turn difficult conversations into purposeful dialogue, positive outcomes, & focused results in 3 easy steps

| 21 |

She was right for a year or so. Nancy kept operating as if the change was impossible. But the impossible happened. The state changed the rules. People like her would no longer be able to do subrogation work. It was set to go into effect a year following the decision.

For Nancy, the news wasn't even a speed bump. She fully expected her firm would be able to continue. With confidence, she assured everyone, "They will change it — I'm sure of it."

When her family and friends pointed out that it was soon to be law throughout the state, she waved them off. "Those companies don't have the staff or time to implement it. Our business is safe." Still she said nothing to the team.

But it wasn't, as she would soon find out.

Over the ensuing year, one by one her clients fell off. Again, people asked about her contingency plan.

She continued to insist she didn't need one. "My clients will be back when they see how much money they are losing. They can't get the skilled people, relationships, or knowledge that we have among us."

"But the law," her family and friends asserted in a unified voice of concerned.

"It will change," she told them with a tone that shut down any opportunity for further discussion.

Nancy carried on without a contingency plan as her savings dwindled by the day. Through it all she remained optimistic despite the growing, desperate pleas from family and friends.

By the end of the year following the passage of the law, Nancy came face-to-face with reality. She had no clients left, no contingencies, and no prospects. Her pipeline was empty and her business dead.

For many months she struggled to face her situation. Eventually, her family had to step in because her money was nearly depleted and she was close to losing her house.

| 22 |

Delivering Bad News in Good Ways:
Turn difficult conversations into purposeful dialogue, positive outcomes, & focused results in 3 easy steps

Nancy had an idealistic, magical mind that fueled her optimism. She had tenacity and bulldog determination. These qualities were among the things that people loved about her.

Nancy's team, family, and friends believed in her wholeheartedly because of the trust she engendered. But she also avoided conflict whenever possible. This resulted in the unfortunate need to let her team go with very little notice.

In the end Nancy bounced back quickly and was on to an entirely new business, as one would expect from someone with her resilience. Her delightful, yet frustrating, magical thinking carried her on to the next venture.

Delivering Bad News in Good Ways:
Turn difficult conversations into purposeful dialogue, positive outcomes, & focused results in 3 easy steps

| 23 |

DON'T BE A NANCY

Reading Nancy's story, it is glaringly obvious there was a problem she needed to address much sooner than she did. As an outsider looking in at a difficult situation like this, it is easy to recognize and determine what to do, but when you are LIVING the situation, it is not quite so easy. Why?

Well, imagine you were in Nancy's shoes.

Often, when faced with doing something we know we need to do but delay or avoid doing it, our mind becomes a veritable obstacle course. It throws up hurdles every time we try.

It is not hard to think of everyday examples of this: starting a new exercise routine, changing eating habits, or ending a relationship. These situations offer that classic conundrum where we think:

"I know it's healthy, good, right, best, but I'm feeling inadequate, afraid, lost, embarrassed, too invested, disingenuous."

We have a story about Nancy as she interacted with others. What we do not have is a view of what was going on inside her head. We are not privy to the inner dialogue, the subconscious rambles that probably play out much like the quote above.

We often unwittingly construct elaborate methods to protect our beliefs about our self and the outside world, as we will explore in Chapter 3.

For now let's consider what could have been going on with Nancy. Maybe you will recognize yourself and others in your professional and personal life as we move through this chapter.

| 24 |

Delivering Bad News in Good Ways:
Turn difficult conversations into purposeful dialogue, positive outcomes, & focused results in 3 easy steps

LURE OF MAGICAL THINKING

We all want to be the one who delivers good news – particularly when it comes to projects. But far too often we find ourselves in the opposite position, which is never fun.

What if the person we have to deliver bad news to is ourselves? We may be tempted to think if we do not acknowledge or look at something painful or difficult, it simply does not exist.

This is the very powerful - and dangerous - lure of wishful, **magical thinking.**

Call it what you like: procrastination, denial, avoidance; magical thinking happens when you pretend that everything will be just fine, even when you are faced with a pile of evidence to the contrary.

The concept can be playful, even fun at times, and it can be useful in some situations. But it is never helpful when it is used to ignore events that will have a negative effect on other people or work projects.

In Nancy's case, there could have been a few reasons that she did not want to acknowledge the changes happening in her industry.

▶ Complacency: She was comfortable in her position and did not want to have to start again

▶ Naiveté: She truly believed things would work out for the best

▶ Ego: She knew she was among the best in her field and could not imagine her clients would not run to her defense rather than replacing her with someone else who also could perform the job

▶ Fear: Concerned this new regulation would harm her business and leave her without the means to support herself, Nancy ignored the possibility because it was simply too frightening to contemplate

It is tempting to delay the delivery of bad news – even to yourself – for as long as possible, but magical thinking almost always ends badly, as it did for Nancy.

Delivering Bad News in Good Ways:
Turn difficult conversations into purposeful dialogue, positive outcomes, & focused results in 3 easy steps

| 25 |

Whether you are a magical thinker or use some other means of avoiding the bad news conversation, the goal is to make sure you do not arrive at a deadline with the work incomplete and wonder how it happened.

Take Nancy's example. She knew what was coming because others talked to her about it. But she refused to take in what they were telling her.

She failed in the first rule of communication: that those on both sides of the conversation hear and understand what the other is saying. This failure does not have to be intentional.

Nancy did not mean to put herself and her employees in financial danger. For some reason, she could not or would not hear (or act on) what she was being told.

MAGICAL THINKING

Magical thinking is never helpful when it is used to avoid events that will have a negative effect on people and projects. We may be tempted to think if we do not acknowledge or look at something painful or difficult, it simply will not exist.

This almost never ends well especially when the situation is littered with clues that something is amiss.

Let's move away from Nancy's story and consider how magical thinking plays out in a more generic workplace scenario.

| 26 |

Delivering Bad News in Good Ways:
Turn difficult conversations into purposeful dialogue, positive outcomes, & focused results in 3 easy steps

YOUR BIG PROJECT FAIL: FEEL IT BEFORE YOU KNOW IT

You have been assigned an important project, and your boss expects it to be complete in three weeks. You know it is going to be a bear to tackle because it involves several decision makers to include the prospective customer on the receiving end of the pitch.

The days slip by and you tell yourself that you just need time to think about it. The days turn into a week. You think you only need a big block of time to sit down and focus on it. You decide the weekend will be the perfect time.

The weekend comes and goes quickly because you had a surprise visit from a friend you have not seen in a long time. You tell yourself it's all good…you will be able to hammer it out over the next week. Of course!

You still have two weeks, you tell yourself. You give it a solid try several times that second week, but you get stuck and find yourself staring at a blank page. Then "luck" steps in when a colleague's project falls through at the last minute, and everyone in the office is pulled in to help.

That steals another three days that you planned to focus on your project. You find yourself feeling slightly relieved as it also offers a diversion from the struggle you are having with your own project.

You begin to feel a slight nagging — you know the feeling. It is that in-between state when you can feel a stir in your stomach that puts your system on mid-level alert that things might be taking a turn for the worst.

But you dismiss the warning as an overreaction. You were built for this. Tales of your superhuman skill at pumping out awesome deliverables at the last minute are the stuff of legend. Yep, no problem popping that proposal out in perfect form — it is nearly baked in the back of your mind even though the actual words elude you.

You are not ready to admit this yet, but what is really tucked in the back of your mind is a boat full of doubt that you can pull it off. You do not know how to get started and feel too much time has gone by to ask for help.

Delivering Bad News in Good Ways:
Turn difficult conversations into purposeful dialogue, positive outcomes, & focused results in 3 easy steps

| 27 |

Your subconscious knows you are embarrassed and afraid, but your conscious mind is not ready to hear all that negative talk. You keep looking ahead like you always do.

Suddenly, you are having trouble sleeping and even more trouble concentrating. You feel overwhelmed by the number of tasks that need your attention, and you cannot seem to prioritize them.

More days slip by and your subconscious decides to up its game. Anxiety is your new constant companion. Anxiety has served humans well since the beginning of time – it alerts us to danger and motivates us to act. The impulse to act lives on a continuum that differs from person to person based on past experience.

To "act" is to do something, and that something can be active or passive. Active in this case would be chucking your ego and asking for help immediately. Passive is to continue to ignore the warning signs and the calendar and tell yourself everything is fine. Shaking it off might be called tenacity.

At this point in the game, many psychologists would call it denial. We will explore that more in Chapter 3.

To do nothing is still an action, even if it seems odd to suggest this. Doing nothing laced with a truckload of justification is avoidance, which will cause trouble.

▶ SO, WHAT TO DO?

The deadline has arrived. The proposal is not done. Stakeholders are expectant. Ignoring the problem instead of working the problem has snowballed into a major threat.

Looking back over the weeks leading up to this point, the physical and mental signs were there. Your mind and body ran the anxiety scale from 1 (mild discomfort) to 10 (catatonic panic).

Butterflies in your stomach, shallow breathing, shakiness, sweat, or maybe headaches gripped you every time you thought about the project. Sometimes physical tugs are accompanied by internal dialogue that could sound like any of these:

| 28 |

Delivering Bad News in Good Ways:
Turn difficult conversations into purposeful dialogue, positive outcomes, & focused results in 3 easy steps

▶ Friend: "You've got plenty of time! No big deal."

▶ Teacher: "Remember that time at school when you put off that research paper? What a disaster!"

▶ Coach: "Come on, you've got this – you always win in the end!"

▶ Parent: "So typical you'd put this off. You know it's your M.O. – just look at your room!"

But for some people there are no voices at all, just crickets...

The trees are still in the forest even if we are not there to see them. And the deadline to submit your proposal is still on the calendar even if it seems really far off, as we will see when we discuss temporal discounting later in this chapter.

There is actually some science to explain the tendency to put off work until deadline is right up on us.

Delivering Bad News in Good Ways:
Turn difficult conversations into purposeful dialogue, positive outcomes, & focused results in 3 easy steps

| 29 |

PROCRASTINATION - A DEEPER LOOK

Scientists define procrastination as the voluntary delay of an action despite foreseeable negative future consequences. It is opting for short-term pleasure at the cost of the long-term.

Sometimes we feel overwhelmed by the task. Sometimes we underestimate the time it will need. Sometimes we feel blah about it. Sometimes we need the urgency that stems from not doing it straight away.

Whatever you are feeling, it is important to note that chronic procrastination is likely an emotional strategy we use for coping with stress.

People may assume anxiety is what prevents them from getting started, yet data from many studies show that for people low in impulsiveness, anxiety is the cue to get going.

Highly impulsive people, on the other hand, shut down when they feel anxiety. Impulsive people are believed to have a harder time dealing with strong emotion and want to do something else to get rid of the bad feeling.

Procrastination not only causes mental stress, but it can cause physical stress. Hypertension, depression, and anxiety are all physically impactful results of putting things off.

The point of this book is not to subject you to deep psychoanalysis to open the crypt of your unconscious. We will consider the psych side only to recognize the things that get in the way of delivering bad news to others. Magical thinking and procrastination certainly fall into that category.

There are ways to address procrastination. These methods require that we are deliberate and disciplined in our approach. This might be difficult at first, but the benefits are worth it. Research supports acknowledging your tendency to procrastinate and imposing deadlines to help you get moving. For more about tips and techniques on this, please check out *www.alisonsigmon.com/resources.*

| 30 |

Delivering Bad News in Good Ways:
Turn difficult conversations into purposeful dialogue, positive outcomes, & focused results in 3 easy steps

SHORT TERM GAIN, LONG TERM LOSS

Humans are reward-driven; we enjoy the shot of dopamine that our bodies give us when we get something we like. This is why we fall into distraction with social media, eating and/or drinking, a good story or video, or even with doing the easy things on our To Do list.

When we complete an easy task or watch a cute baby goat video we get a dopamine buzz from that happy brain chemical when we have completed something.

But a long-term project leaves us to wonder whether we will get a payoff at the end. Maybe we will, and maybe we won't. In the meantime, the hours and days slip by.

While we opt in and enjoy the immediate gratification of short-term successes, we are actually delaying the inevitable - the suffering we will likely experience because we are not any closer to finishing that big project or delivering that bad news.

The tendency to over- or under-estimate the value of a reward based on how close we perceive it is called **temporal discounting.** This phenomenon is discussed in research literature as far back as 1937 according to Soman, et al, in their paper titled *The Psychology of Intertemporal Discounting: Why are Distant Events Valued Differently from Proximal Ones?*

Researchers say that if the payoff is immediate, then we tend to take it and move on even if waiting gives us a bigger gain. A famous example is if you offer $100 now or $110 in a month, most people opt for the $100 now — they do not want to wait.

The flip side of this is something called **hyperbolic discounting.** If you offer $100 a year from now or $110 in a year plus a month from now, people tend to wait for the $110 because they think "what's one more month when I've already waited a year?" Basically, the more distant the reward, the more inclined we are to think it is not as valuable or such a big deal.

How does this play into Nancy's scenario? What she did is not surprising, given how the human brain works. It was not a good business practice, which

Delivering Bad News in Good Ways:
Turn difficult conversations into purposeful dialogue, positive outcomes, & focused results in 3 easy steps

| 31 |

is why you need to be able to recognize symptoms of bad news and act on it as soon as possible, even when it is uncomfortable or scary or feels far in the future.

In project management this is an example of the risk-issue relationship. We define the symptoms of risks and check them regularly to prevent them from becoming issues. Nancy ignored this.

She knew, intellectually, that doing nothing in the face of the rule changes in her field meant that she would one day lose her business. But a year seemed like such a long time in the future. And in the short-term, there was still work to be done and money to be made. Besides, accepting the bad news that her business was at risk was VERY unpleasant.

So Nancy accepted today's reward (growing clientele and profit) and discounted the long-term reward (discovering and launching another type of business) until it was nearly too late.

In the next chapter, we will take a deeper look at what drives behavior like Nancy's and why we have a hard time dealing with and sharing bad news.

CHAPTER TAKEAWAYS

▶ Pitfalls of magical thinking

▶ Physical effects of stress

▶ Why we procrastinate

▶ Risk/reward drive

▶ Temporal and hyperbolic discounting

| 32 |

Delivering Bad News in Good Ways:
Turn difficult conversations into purposeful dialogue, positive outcomes, & focused results in 3 easy steps

CHAPTER 3:

WHY IS IT SO TOUGH TO DELIVER BAD NEWS?

OH, THE PLACES WE GO WITH OUR STORIES (FEARS)

"GIVE ME A SHOT. I CAN'T ADDRESS WHAT I'M NOT AWARE OF."

Brian's back stiffened, and his voice stepped up an octave as Lana asked yet again what he had been saying behind her back. She actually knew what he had said; several people had shared the stories with her.

A day earlier, one of Lana's teammates said Brian had issues with some of her decisions. The teammate continued with saying, "Since he arrived a week ago, he's made it clear he doesn't agree with how you set things up here."

The team had been in the field for nearly a month for the third time in six months. This was Brian's first time out with them. No one knew him well, but he arrived with a reputation for being sharp and efficient. When Lana's teammate approached her with news that Brian had been criticizing her to the team, she knew the situation needed to be addressed quickly.

They were collecting data for a series of tests to assess the performance of new military equipment under consideration for a multi-year purchase starting the following year.

The equipment would require the retirement of an aging, expensive model which meant a sizable budget would be needed to purchase the equipment, train people to use it, and sunset the old equipment. The project was so large that it required congressional approval so the team needed to ensure the data was solid.

A lot was riding on this. Lana needed all hands and brains on deck and that included Brian. If he had input, the team needed it.

She asked herself repeatedly why he didn't feel he could speak up directly to her. In her mind, if there was a problem that needed to be addressed then get on with it or the group would stand to suffer. She believed his perspective, as with other team members, was important and he needed to know that. He also needed to understand the passive aggressive talk could kill a team in a heartbeat.

She checked his schedule and approached him off duty. When Lana found him, she let him know she had heard through the grapevine that he had some issues with the decisions she had made about how she had set up the test site.

"No, no, everything's fine," he said with some urgency.

She recounted a few of the specifics she had been provided and said in a calm, non-threatening manner, "Brian, it's okay. You are an expert in your field and I respect that. I want to hear your perspective."

Again he said with a hint of anxiousness, "No, really…everything is okay on my end."

Clearly it was not, she thought, or they would not be having this conversation.

Lana was at a crossroads. She sincerely wanted to hear his perspective, but something was blocking him. Then it occurred to her that he probably never had a good experience in his career with providing feedback or giving what he perceived as bad news to management. It was likely he had been put down, punished in some way, or marginalized.

She made a decision right then. As he stood there with his back stiff and sweat beads forming on his brow looking like he was about to start another round of saying nothing was wrong, she decided she had two goals in this conversation:

1. Get him to share and explore his feedback

2. Make this a good experience with management so he would be more willing to open up sooner in the future instead of going behind the person's back

Looking at him squarely and sincerely, she said, "Obviously, we are of a different mind. That's okay. If you have thoughts on how we can improve our processes and functions, the team deserves that opportunity.

"Give me a shot. I can't address what I'm not aware of."

Delivering Bad News in Good Ways:
Turn difficult conversations into purposeful dialogue, positive outcomes, & focused results in 3 easy steps

| 35 |

It took a couple of minutes, but then he finally opened up. The more he spoke, the more relaxed he became in response to Lana listening intently and asking him questions.

Over the next 45 minutes they discussed the issue and their respective perspectives. Lana thought Brian had some good points. After hearing her side of things, he said he understood why she made the decisions she made at the test site. She told him she appreciated his ideas and let him know the changes they could make in response.

By the end of the discussion, they both felt more enlightened and said as much. Lana reiterated the need for him to come to her directly in the future so they could continue to improve. He agreed. From that point forward, Brian became a committed advocate to Lana and the team.

| 36 |

Delivering Bad News in Good Ways:
Turn difficult conversations into purposeful dialogue, positive outcomes, & focused results in 3 easy steps

DON'T BE A BRIAN

Brian struggled to confront Lana directly and instead went behind her back, which put the integrity and functioning of the team at risk. Lana could have assumed a defensive, avoidant, or authoritarian position, but she did not do any of those things.

Instead she chose to investigate and gather the facts to help her evaluate and determine the best way to approach the situation. These two steps – the Separate and Evaluate steps in the SED model we will explore in further detail in Chapters 5 and 6 – were critical to gaining Brian's trust and to shoring up a team culture of openness and collaboration.

She knew it was not just about Brian and his behavior. It was also about the team. They were in the middle of a long, high profile project and the last thing they needed was to be distracted by behavior that would undermine their effectiveness.

Over time Lana learned her hunch was correct about the reasons behind Brian's actions in the early stage of joining the team. He admitted that a recent bad experience with a supervisor had left him feeling raw. He feared speaking up would continue to strain relations with his supervisor if word got back to him about this situation.

Fear of retribution drove his behavior, and in the end he saw how fear-driven behavior potentially jeopardized the entire operation.

Let's take a look at what can drive this.

Delivering Bad News in Good Ways:
Turn difficult conversations into purposeful dialogue, positive outcomes, & focused results in 3 easy steps

| 37 |

WHAT GETS IN THE WAY

Okay, I will come clean. This is actually a variation of a real event from a project in which I was involved during my time in the military. I did not realize it at the time, but even back then I was working on SED.

So, why is it hard to deliver bad news?

Fear of retribution, as in Brian's case, is one reason. Other reasons may include:

▶ Burden of responsibility

▶ Not wanting to cause pain or be that "bad" or "hurtful" person

▶ Lack of skill

▶ Limited language/terminology

▶ Low confidence

▶ Doubt

▶ Fear of inadequacy or making mistakes

▶ Anticipation of rejection

▶ Not knowing how to deal with the other person's response

▶ "Fatal flaw" – fallacy thinking

Whatever the reasons that hold a person back, in my experience it comes down to three key ideas:

1. I don't want to hurt you

2. I don't want to be hurt

3. I don't know how

| 38 |

Delivering Bad News in Good Ways:
Turn difficult conversations into purposeful dialogue, positive outcomes, & focused results in 3 easy steps

I DON'T WANT TO HURT YOU

Psychology has given us a wide range of concepts to explain our need to protect our emotional selves. Behavior is driven by experiences and those experiences make us effective, ineffective, or stagnant.

We can intellectually understand our ineffective patterns and learn more effective methods for avoiding them, but that is just half the battle. **The other half is actually using them in the heat of the moment.**

Behavior is reinforced through repetition and experience. It takes about two weeks of practice for a new concept or behavior to take root. So practice is key.

Another key to reinforcing new learning is to have some understanding of the emotional gains we get from the way our past self dealt with a similar situation. Yep...you read that sentence right.

We receive something from the old way we have done things. It feeds some emotional need, which makes it hard to change behavior even when logic tells you it is the right thing to do. The head might be all for it, but if the heart's not in it then the attempt will likely fizzle.

So, if we are not aware of what drives our behavior when it comes to delivering bad news then we risk slipping back into old, familiar responses.

The key to avoiding your "old" response is recognizing when you are about to do it and talking yourself back from the edge. This is what Lana had to do – oh wait, yep, that was me so let me own it.

▶ HOW DID I FEEL IN THAT SITUATION?
I felt offended and angry when I heard that Brian (name changed) had said negative things about my ideas behind my back. My first thought was to attack, but I did not do so.

I gave myself a pause. I figuratively counted to ten and pulled myself back from the edge. I knew reacting would feed my craving for revenge, but in the long run that response would undermine and even unhinge the team.

Delivering Bad News in Good Ways:
Turn difficult conversations into purposeful dialogue, positive outcomes, & focused results in 3 easy steps

| 39 |

That ability does not just happen. It takes awareness, identification of a replacement behavior/process, motivation to use the replacement behavior, and practice. Oh, and lots of deep breathing.

It is tempting to just keep doing what we know. What we know is so deeply ingrained in our mind and body that we are often unaware of falling back on old behavior when we do it. Like poet laureate Maya Angelou's grandmother reportedly used to say, "When you know better, you do better."

It is true we have the opportunity to do better, but to be successful in doing better we need to have some insight into the beliefs and behaviors that might work against us in the process.

Whether you hesitate to deliver bad news because you don't want to hurt others, don't want to be hurt, or don't know how to do it, the underpinnings of these reasons probably lead to a fear that is likely a theme in your life.

While not a business example, I think the following personal story makes this point.

When I was around 10 years old, I had a friend who I found rather captivating. She was cute, fun, and carefree. She also had very cool toys. She had one in particular — a Barbie camper — something I had wanted for quite a while.

For about a week or two, my friend and I talked at school about her toys and her bringing them to my house for a sleepover on the weekend. I reminded her repeatedly not to forget to bring the Barbie camper! I loved this toy and privately envied her for having it. I did not realize it at the time, but I had an ulterior motive for hounding her about bringing it to my house.

Finally the day arrived, and as promised, she brought along her toys and the highly prized Barbie camper. We played and had a great time during our sleepover. I could not get enough of the camper and my gracious friend let me dominate it.

During that weekend I recall having moments when I hoped she might forget it at my house so I would have more time to play with it.

When her mother arrived to pick her up, we gathered up her belongings to load into the car. We had to make a few trips and her mother was pressed for time. In the hustle of collecting everything quickly, chances were high that something was going to be missed.

| 40 |

Delivering Bad News in Good Ways:
Turn difficult conversations into purposeful dialogue, positive outcomes, & focused results in 3 easy steps

And guess just what got missed...

The much-adored Barbie camper was overlooked. I discovered it as her mother backed the car out of the driveway. I ran to the driveway with the toy in hand, but with each step I slowed my pace.

By the time I reached the driveway, they were already moving down the road. I looked down at it in my hands and felt a tinge of guilt for not trying harder to catch them before they left. That feeling evaporated with the realization that I would have more time to play with it!

Over the next few days I blissfully immersed myself in grand story play with the camper as the main prop. When I saw her at school, I thought about mentioning it to her but never got around to it.

As the days passed, I felt less and less good about playing with it. I thought about calling her to arrange to return it, but then did not out of growing shame and embarrassment.

Although I had not stolen the toy, it began to feel like it the longer I avoided the subject. I told myself I didn't bring it up with her because I didn't want to hurt her.

It took a few weeks, but I finally mentioned the toy to my mother who made sure it was returned to my friend. The guilt I felt over the situation made me pull back from our friendship. I feared if she knew the truth, which I grew to recognize as deception, she would reject me for not being honest about my intentions.

We never talked about it again and afterward we drifted apart. Perhaps we drifted away from each other because young relationships like that tend to be fleeting, but to my young mind, it was because of my behavior.

That fear of rejection and being regarded as a bad person is alive and well today. It still crops up in my inner dialogue especially when it comes to telling people something I think will create anger or rejection.

Why does this keep cropping up? Let's find out...

Delivering Bad News in Good Ways:
Turn difficult conversations into purposeful dialogue, positive outcomes, & focused results in 3 easy steps

| 41 |

FEAR REFRAMED: THE GREAT TEACHER

In 2012, writer Karen Thomas Walker filmed a simple but powerful TED Talk called *What Fear Can Teach Us.*

Instead of seeing fear as a weakness, she suggests we consider fear as a resource, a teacher. She continues:

"...we all know what it's like to be afraid. We know how fear feels, but I'm not sure we spend enough time thinking about what our fears mean."

To illustrate her point, she recounts the story of the whaleship Essex, which was part of the inspiration for Herman Melville's Moby Dick.

It was the 1800s and 20 American sailors were 3,000 miles off the coast of Chile when their ship was struck by a sperm whale. With water flooding the ship, the crew evacuated to small whaleboats, which had limited supplies and very basic navigation equipment.

The sailors were now adrift, and the situation was dire. No one knew about the accident. No one would come looking for them any time soon. Supplies on hand required they reach land as soon as possible. They considered their options:

▶ Attempt to reach the Marquesas Islands, which were 1,200 miles away

▶ Sail north for Hawaii

▶ Head 1,500 miles south hoping to reach winds that may push them towards the South American coast

None of the three options was great. The islands were rumored to be inhabited by cannibals, the route to Hawaii plagued with storms during that time of year, and the South American coast was risky because of insufficient supplies for the time it would take.

Fear danced in their imaginations: Eaten by cannibals, battered by storms, or starve before reaching land. Likely as they deliberated options, intricate, plot-filled, visually stimulating stories emerged. To Walker's point when asking what our fears mean, try swapping the word "fear" for the word "story."

| 42 |

Delivering Bad News in Good Ways:
Turn difficult conversations into purposeful dialogue, positive outcomes, & focused results in 3 easy steps

In my toy example, my young mind felt fear and that fear created stories and those stories drove my actions. So, too, did it for Brian and for the sailors. I lost a friendship, Brian nearly lost his position on the team, and the sailors? Well, ironically, the sailors ended up experiencing the very thing they feared the most.

Fears (oops! stories) weave many outcome possibilities. But, why do we chose one over other options? What drives that? Well, we will dive deeper into that in Chapter 5 and Chapter 6, but for now we can look at it as the marriage of art and science.

When reading our fears (stories), as Walker notes the famed novelist Vladimir Nabokov said, we need to have an artist's passion to let go and get caught up in the story experience, but we also need a scientist's "coolness of judgment" to question and temper our assumptions.

The problem we bump into with the narratives our wonderful imagination provides us?

If we only have the artist's passion in play, we risk giving in to the most vivid and lurid narrative just like Brian, the sailors, and I did in our respective situations. Why? Simply put, it is the easiest and requires little effort.

Our minds tend to gravitate to the most overt, extreme, and outlandish because it is so stimulating. This is why we love those talking dog videos (it's so crazy they can do that, right?!?) or slow down to gawk if there is a car accident - it is so extreme, different, or incongruent with our experience that it catches our attention.

Slow-boil events like heart disease, clogged arteries, and climate change simply do not offer that adrenaline punch so those real threats, as Walker pointed out in her Ted Talk, tend to get passed over until they become urgent.

Fears spawn irrational thoughts AND irrational thoughts feed fears. And now we run the risk of creating a self-filling prophecy.

And this is where things have the potential to really go off the rails, as we will see.

Delivering Bad News in Good Ways:
Turn difficult conversations into purposeful dialogue, positive outcomes, & focused results in 3 easy steps

| 43 |

"I DON'T WANT TO HURT YOU" IS ALSO "I DON'T WANT TO HURT"

Just like in Karen Thomas Walker's TED Talk about fear as a teacher, irrational beliefs and defenses are good teachers as well. I will assume the role of Captain Obvious here - in case you have not noticed, fear, irrational beliefs, and defenses are all loosely connected. Let's start with irrational thinking. Here's a definition for you from Wikipedia:

*Irrationality is cognition, **thinking,** talking or acting without inclusion of rationality. It is more specifically described as an action or opinion given through inadequate use of reason, emotional distress, or cognitive deficiency.*

Irrational thoughts and beliefs often fuel magical thinking, discussed in Chapter 2, and vice versa. They light up our fears, in turn, creating imaginative, unfounded stories like what happened with the crew of the whaleship Essex. You guessed it...we all are great fiction writers.

Irrational thoughts and beliefs have little to no data to support them. Basically, we tend to make decisions based on the baggage we collect from past experiences. We saw this in Brian's story.

Albert Ellis, renowned psychologist and developer of **Rational Emotive Therapy,** identified a list of dysfunctional beliefs we typically have rolling around in our heads.

See if you can relate to any of them by some degree. You can assign a number on a scale from one to 10 with one being the least and 10 being the most. Imagine them on a continuum. Consider what situations you have experienced in the past that intensified the ones to which you most relate.

When the situation intensifies, it is more challenging to be objective particularly when delivering bad news and having the conversation that follows it.

▸ It is a dire necessity for adult humans to be loved or approved by virtually every significant other person in their community.

| 44 |

Delivering Bad News in Good Ways:
Turn difficult conversations into purposeful dialogue, positive outcomes, & focused results in 3 easy steps

- One absolutely must be competent, adequate, and achieving in all important respects or else one is an inadequate, worthless person.

- People absolutely must act considerately and fairly and they are damnable villains if they do not. They are their bad acts.

- It is awful and terrible when things are not the way one would very much like them to be.

- Emotional disturbance is mainly externally caused and people have little or no ability to increase or decrease their dysfunctional feelings and behaviors.

- If something is or may be dangerous or fearsome, then one should be constantly and excessively concerned about it and should keep dwelling on the possibility of it occurring.

- One cannot and must not face life's responsibilities and difficulties and it is easier to avoid them.

- One's past history is an all-important determiner of one's present behavior and because something once strongly affected one's life, it should indefinitely have a similar effect.

- Other people's disturbances are horrible and one must feel upset about them.

- There is invariably a right, precise and perfect solution to human problems and it is awful if this perfect solution is not found.

Ellis's beliefs are deliberately extreme and polarized, to highlight that we often take exaggerated viewpoints that require little thought (remember the crew of the whaleship Essex!).

He called this extreme approach "awfulizing." We tend to do this when we have a strong need for certainty in a situation (hint, hint...we crave control in the face of the unfamiliar, confusing, hurtful).

What is the irony in such cases? The extreme that keeps us locked in a certain way of thinking may be counterproductive to what we say we want or need. For example, we remain in a job that we hate, we live in an area that is uninspiring, or we stay in a relationship that is unhealthy.

Delivering Bad News in Good Ways:
Turn difficult conversations into purposeful dialogue, positive outcomes, & focused results in 3 easy steps

| 45 |

We complain about these things but we don't DO anything about them.

Staying in the situation we complain about actually provides identity and gives us something to talk about with others. (I just heard myself say "Uh-oh…" Maybe you said it to yourself, too.) We actually get attention from "awfulizing," and it can even be a point of connection with others who are experiencing something similar.

Okay, so we have got the irrational bit. What keeps those thoughts in lockstep with our preferred view? Defenses, like good foot soldiers, are eager to serve.

| 46 |

Delivering Bad News in Good Ways:
Turn difficult conversations into purposeful dialogue, positive outcomes, & focused results in 3 easy steps

DEFENSE MECHANISMS: FRIEND AND FOE

Psychologists have given us a host of words to explain behavior that protects us from feeling hurt, threatened, et cetera – they are called defense mechanisms.

Now, before you skip ahead with an "oh, brother" attitude, hang in for a second.

Defense mechanisms protect us from thinking about or dealing with things that feel threatening – no, not physically threatening – emotionally threatening. To be fair, not all defense mechanisms are bad. It just depends on how they are used.

Awareness of your go-to defenses helps you assess if they are helping you or getting in your way, particularly when it comes to delivering bad news.

Here are a few defense mechanisms with examples of how they are used.

Can you see yourself in any? Which ones? Can you imagine an emotional gain from using your go-to response?

▶ **Displacement:** Yelling at your mate, children, or dog after learning your boss killed your project

▶ **Sublimation:** Instead of yelling at your mate, children, or dog after your boss killed your project, you go for a run or a kickboxing class (this is a good one!)

▶ **Denial:** Not accepting that your boss killed your project, you simply carry on with it as if the cancellation never happened

▶ **Avoidance:** For days you have not responded to repeated calls, texts, and emails from your boss, nor did you try to contact her to talk about the status of the project

▶ **Projection:** You think your boss killed your project because she does not like you, when the truth is you do not like her very much

▶ **Intellectualization:** After learning your boss killed your project, you dive into the facts, figures, and reports for several days losing sleep and

Delivering Bad News in Good Ways:
Turn difficult conversations into purposeful dialogue, positive outcomes, & focused results in 3 easy steps

| 47 |

skipping meals in your quest for more information

▶ **Rationalization:** You blame management that the project failed instead of considering that your inexperience with the subject or your less than present performance might be a contributing factor

▶ **Regression:** Upon hearing the boss killed your project, you complain about "how inept management is" to anyone who will listen

▶ **Reaction Formation:** Your boss is solemn and grim when she tells you she killed the project. Your response is to smile and speak sweetly, even though you are fuming inside.

▶ **Passive-aggressive:** Anticipating that your boss will kill the project, you subtly start mentioning to colleagues that some of the things your boss did on the project "didn't make sense" and you would never have done it like that

▶ **Withdrawal:** You call in sick several days in a row after your boss asks you to get on her calendar to discuss the performance issues on your project

In the toy example, I used avoidance to protect my emotional self and my friend (or so I told myself) from feeling pain. That is how defense mechanisms work. They protect us from feeling pain.

In some cases that is helpful and healthy because there are some situations that require a bit more emotional development, skill, and capacity to tackle. But there are times when a defense mechanism is not healthy in business or in life.

This is when we get in our own way.

Let's take a page from the creative writing world. In her article titled *The Fatal Flaw - The Most Essential Element for Bringing Characters to Life,* Dara Marks, Ph.D., provides a solid definition of character fatal flaw and the transformation opportunity it creates:

"The FATAL FLAW is a struggle within a character to maintain a survival system long after it has outlived its usefulness … In order to create a story that expresses the arc of transformation, a need for that transformation must be established."

| 48 |

Delivering Bad News in Good Ways:
Turn difficult conversations into purposeful dialogue, positive outcomes, & focused results in 3 easy steps

It is the fatal flaw that creates an opportunity for change and growth. Without it there is no need do anything different. You might be wondering why we are using literary and theatrical concepts in a book like this. Well, as we know, art imitates life. Remember, we all are great fiction writers.

Just like a character in a story, we have patterns of behavior — some helpful, others not so much. It is the "not so much" that creates opportunities for transformation, but that only occurs if what we are doing is not meeting our needs, internally or externally.

In other words, something challenges our tendency to cruise in status quo mode. It motivates us to step outside our comfort zone because we encounter something more meaningful than our emotional protection and self-preservation.

Delivering Bad News in Good Ways:
Turn difficult conversations into purposeful dialogue, positive outcomes, & focused results in 3 easy steps

| 49 |

THE WHISTLE OF TRANSFORMATION BLOWS

What does it take for our own transformation? What is enough to motivate people to step outside their comfort zones?

A higher profile example of this is in the case of a whistleblower. The whistleblower's task is to deliver potentially extreme bad news because it will likely impact many people and could have devastating repercussions. Whistleblowers sideline their pain and risk their emotional safety for the greater good of the affected group.

To illustrate this I am reminded of someone I met many years ago when teaching a series of project management courses for a large bank. The individual, who we will call Jason, told me he had worked for the bank for more than 15 years, but that was not where his career began.

Jason said he landed his dream job working in the energy sector right out of college. He loved the business and earned rapid promotion and increasing responsibility for his energy, deep skill set, and innovative ability.

Popular with colleagues and management, he fully expected to make it a lifelong career. He embraced the company, people, and structure saying the he had fully "drunk the Kool-Aid."

Several years passed. He got married, had children, played on the company softball team, and continued to enjoy increasing responsibility and fatter paychecks. One day his supervisor called him aside to discuss some safety procedures and operational processes for which Jason had been responsible and had recently completed a series of tests.

Apparently, some test results did not quite turn out as expected, which would cost a great deal of time and money to address. His supervisor explained the situation to Jason, emphasizing the adverse impact the results would have "up the chain."

Jason's boss feared budget cuts and layoffs as a result. The supervisor said the results were so close to qualifying for passing that he felt it would be fine to "call it good."

| 50 |

Delivering Bad News in Good Ways:
Turn difficult conversations into purposeful dialogue, positive outcomes, & focused results in 3 easy steps

Jason listened deeply and intently. As his boss spoke, Jason's inner voice kept chanting, "Please don't ask me to do what I think you're going to ask me to do." But then the supervisor asked it – the thing Jason did not want to hear. He asked Jason to change the numbers on the test to a passing grade.

Jason said nothing. The supervisor told him to go home and think about it. "I would sure hate for your future, our future here to be put at stake," the supervisor said as Jason walked away.

Jason thought carefully about the implications. Not agreeing to the request threatened his financial security and continued promotion in a company he dearly loved. With two young children and another on the way, a recently purchased house, and a single income, he felt unnerved – no, physically sick, he told me, in response.

Then he considered the other side of his dilemma. Agreeing to change the results could put his colleagues at risk, as well as hundreds of thousands of company customers.

When he returned to work the next day, he told his supervisor he could not and would not do it. He said, "I simply couldn't compromise my values nor could I do something that would cause harm to others."

Nothing happened for a while. Then, over the next few months, his performance reports were downgraded even though he had done nothing different except refuse to comply with the supervisor's request.

"Eventually," he said, devoid of any emotion, "I was fired. I knew it was coming, so I had some time to prepare."

He finished his story with, "That was 15 years ago. I've been at this bank ever since. If I had it to do all over again, I would do exactly the same thing. In my exit interview from that company, I shared the truth about what happened. After I left, I heard they got someone to fudge the numbers. It did cause a problem and that company, after a string of even bigger ethical missteps, no longer exists."

Delivering Bad News in Good Ways:
Turn difficult conversations into purposeful dialogue, positive outcomes, & focused results in 3 easy steps

| 51 |

WHY GIVING BAD NEWS CAN LITERALLY HURT

Over the years I have had a lot conversations with people — and my share of experiences — with giving bad news. The general consensus seems to be that we all prefer a root canal without anesthesia to giving bad news.

What is it about delivering bad news that makes it so tough?

While everyone experiences such events differently, there is some science behind the struggle.

So consider this...

Have you ever walked away from a major stakeholder meeting feeling confident everyone was aligned and enthusiastic about a new project only to learn later they hate the idea and are quietly withdrawing support even though you are still on the hook for it?" **Ouch.**

Remember that time when you worked so hard on a proposal, project plan, design, or research paper, and it was ripped to shreds by others? **Really??? How could they not see the brilliance you slaved to create?**

How did you feel when you had to tell a sponsor of a project or perhaps a loved one something you knew would likely throw the project, a team, or life into a tailspin? **Need Ibuprofen and a bed. Now.**

All of us have had professional and personal situations where we had to give and receive bad news. Whether giver or receiver, any sentient being will feel it and in some cases they literally feel it — that is, researchers have found the experience can be felt as real physical pain.

Most people can vividly recount moments as children and adults where they experienced rejection or what was perceived as rejection. In describing the event, they often include physical responses such as gagging, stomach ache, headache, and shallow breathing as examples.

The pain associated with those experiences can be so intense and deeply felt that the person may feel paralyzed and lost. This can trigger all kinds of defenses.

| 52 |

Delivering Bad News in Good Ways:
Turn difficult conversations into purposeful dialogue, positive outcomes, & focused results in 3 easy steps

As noted in the article *Psychologists: Physical and Social Pain Hurts the Same Way*

by Christine Hsu, researchers found that people who are more sensitive to physical pain typically experience social pain and rejection more acutely. And to add yet another twist to the findings, when these people were given Tylenol for three weeks, they experienced less emotional pain.

The study did not say if giving or receiving bad news got any easier. I imagine that part does not change. It likely comes down to how we cope with it internally and how we manage it with others.

To understand why giving bad news can be difficult, ask yourself a few things:

▶ What kind of reaction in the past did your boss, an authority figure, or someone you care about have to bad news?

▶ How did you physically feel in response to their reaction?

▶ What did you do to get past negative memories so you could move toward a solution to the problem?

▶ As a kid, when you saw one adult giving bad news to another adult, how did they take it? Anger, withdrawal, sadness? What did that feel like to you? Good, bad, scary, threatening?

▶ What does "rejection" mean to you? If you are giving bad news, is the other person's response really rejection of you or are your emotions influencing your interpretation?

▶ How can you stay focused on the situation and not let the "pain" of delivery and response get in the way?

▶ What stories/fears pop up for you in anticipation of sharing bad news?

Once we have insight into why we respond as we do (stomach ache, headache, anger, mean words, blame, defensiveness, withdrawal, freezing up, or passing it off to someone else), then we can get a grip on managing our internal responses. This will free us to focus on finding solutions faster.

Delivering Bad News in Good Ways:
Turn difficult conversations into purposeful dialogue, positive outcomes, & focused results in 3 easy steps

| 53 |

I DON'T KNOW HOW

Well, "I don't know how" is why I wrote this book and why you are reading it. I have a hunch that you have the basics already.

We are just going to organize it, give you some terms so you can gut check it, and practice it so you will feel more confident in your ability to manage that scared/nervous/anxious reactive inner voice with a compassionate, caring, and focused voice of action.

Delivering bad news is a triumph over our own pain and discomfort. It is a path to greater good when shared with compassion and purpose. We begin building our worldview constructs from the cradle and hone our defenses to keep that worldview and our emotional selves in check as we roll through life.

Defense mechanisms are designed to protect us, but that does not mean we do not need checks and balances to ensure they do not get in our way.

Processes like the **SED Method** are among the techniques to ensure checks and balances are place.

Let's turn to Chapter 4 for an overview of the SED Method.

CHAPTER TAKEAWAYS

- ▶ What gets in the way of delivering bad news
- ▶ Defense mechanisms
- ▶ Irrational thinking
- ▶ Fatal Flaw
- ▶ Transformation
- ▶ Pain and giving bad news

| 54 |

Delivering Bad News in Good Ways:
Turn difficult conversations into purposeful dialogue, positive outcomes, & focused results in 3 easy steps

CHAPTER 4:

WELCOME TO THE SED METHOD

OVERVIEW OF THE SED TOOL FOR DELIVERY: SEPARATE, EVALUATE, & DELIVER

"...ONE OF THE GREATEST ACHIEVEMENTS OF OUR TIME"

It was a big year. In 1979, Mattel released a video game console called Intellivision and Activision was founded as the first third-party video game developer. Thirty-two year old Bill Clinton was sworn in as Arkansas governor, Ronald Reagan announced his U.S. presidential candidacy, and Margaret Thatcher became the first female prime minister of Great Britain.

The Los Angeles Lakers selected number one draft pick Magic Johnson, Muhammad Ali announced his retirement, and the Steelers took the Cowboys in Super Bowl XIII. The year was also dominated by a gas shortage, the hostage crisis, and the Iranian revolution.

There was a lot going on that year, not the least of which was the Egypt-Israel Peace Treaty negotiations facilitated by U.S. President Jimmy Carter. Carter had a tough go of it with his presidency from the very beginning.

One of his first actions as president was taking on two bloated government agencies that spent money on building dams that the U.S. did not need or want. Those agencies fought back hard, and as a result Carter had a tough time pushing his other interests through congress.

Carter needed a win and with the Egypt-Israel Peace Treaty negotiations, which sought Israel's withdrawal from the Sinai Peninsula and the restoration of "normal friendly relations" between Egypt and Israel, he had a shot at it.

It was well known that President Anwar el-Sadat of Egypt did not like Prime Minister Menachem Begin of Israel, and both men had deep differences politically and personally.

Inviting them to Camp David, Carter carefully moved the two leaders beyond their respective differences to embrace the larger mission and responsibility of peace for people living in the Middle East.

The first few days of the thirteen-day accord were described as a "screaming match." At one point it got so bad between them that Sadat and Begin had to be physically separated.

| 56 |

Delivering Bad News in Good Ways:
Turn difficult conversations into purposeful dialogue, positive outcomes, & focused results in 3 easy steps

Because of the strained relationship, Carter had to help the two leaders see past their differences and the intense emotions that fueled them to address the real problems the region and the world would face if they could not find common ground.

That was no small feat, but in the end he was able to do it. Afterward, Sadat reportedly said that Carter's effort "constitutes one of the greatest achievements of our time."

Most of us will never be in negotiations that have a world impact such as this, but we all will bump into situations where personalities, beliefs, and values will not line up with our own.

Whether aware of it or not, people have feelings and will hold tight to those feelings even when contrary evidence is presented. This is a particular risk when delivering bad news.

The trick is to use a process that can help you assess your feelings, anticipate the feelings of others, evaluate and communicate options, and negotiate next steps.

This is what we will do using SED Method. It is a trial and error, reactionary behavior replacement that will help you do the prep work needed to share bad news. This chapter provides an overview of the SED Method; chapters 5-7 give deeper details for each step.

Once the prep work is complete, we will then use the Talk model, which is covered in Chapter 8, to provide a touchstone to navigate and negotiate in the conversation that follows.

Let's dive into the method overview…

Delivering Bad News in Good Ways:
Turn difficult conversations into purposeful dialogue, positive outcomes, & focused results in 3 easy steps

| 57 |

SED METHOD OVERVIEW: SEPARATE, EVALUATE, & DELIVER

The right word may be effective, but no word was ever as effective as a rightly timed pause. ~ Mark Twain

A principle noted in the Roger Fisher and William Ury book called G*etting to Yes: Negotiating Agreement Without Giving In* states that negotiators should "separate the people from the problem." Carter demonstrated this principle during the Egypt-Israel Peace Treaty negotiations.

The same principle applies to delivering bad news, but this is a little trickier than it may seem. Project support is driven from some level of emotional investment. Contrary to popular belief and supported by research, there is a point when the paycheck is not what compels us to do our best in our work.

Whether we are driven to help others, innovate, learn a new skill, collaborate, or earn recognition, all are fueled by emotional investment. With studies from groups like Gallup, we are learning that intrinsic rewards (personal interest, enjoying a task, learning growth) are much stronger motivators in the workplace than extrinsic rewards (pay, benefits, stock options).

Whatever the source, every project manager and team manager hopes to have that level of passion and commitment on the team, BUT it comes with a price. The higher the emotional investment people have in their work or project, the harder time they will have bouncing back from bad news about it.

MOVING AT THE SPEED OF LIGHT

With the evolution of technology and more than 3 billion people worldwide using the Internet, today's business climate requires quick change to stay viable. The speed, reach, and consumer options available mean organizations must be nimble, creative, and able to adjust quickly to shifting market conditions.

The upside of the ability to change quickly is market edge, but the downside is that change impacts people in their day-to-day work, which can be perceived by stakeholders as bad, difficult, or challenging. Communicating change to

| 58 |

Delivering Bad News in Good Ways:
Turn difficult conversations into purposeful dialogue, positive outcomes, & focused results in 3 easy steps

stakeholders is a daily occurrence for project managers.

So why is it so hard for stakeholders to get past "bad" and just get the work done?

According to David Brooks in his book, **The Social Animal,** the globalization paradigm means information can move 15,000 miles instantly. That means people are hit with roughly 11 trillion (that's nine zeros) bits of information at once, but are lucky to have awareness of maybe 40 of them at one time.

Lisa Cron in her book **Wired for Story** notes research that found that when it comes to actually paying attention to those bits of information, we are likely only able to actively, deeply understand five to seven in a day.

Richard A. Block, Peter A. Hancock, and Dan Zakay in their article titled *How cognitive load affects duration judgments: A meta-analytic review,* state that it is a phenomenon called cognitive load paradigm that contributes to people being unable to adapt to change as rapidly as technology evolves and changes.

So, the net-net is it takes time for people to adapt to the change that companies need for projects to be delivered quickly. While helpful with project buy-in and commitment, throwing emotional investment into the mix can further slow response and even create backlash.

Anvi and her product development team experienced something like this on their technology project, as noted in the story below.

Anvi was excited. As the lead product designer and now business side project manager for a major Internet product development project, her team would finally get to see the results of their yearlong research and design efforts. After a competitive vendor selection process to support the development of the system, they were thrilled with their vendor partner, who brought a ton of valuable system experience to the table.

They began work immediately on the design review and specs. After countless meetings to vet the requirements and months of reviews and changes, the team landed on an architecture design that would make the system scalable and manageable.

Delivering Bad News in Good Ways:
Turn difficult conversations into purposeful dialogue, positive outcomes, & focused results in 3 easy steps

| 59 |

Over those months, Anvi lined up resources, worked with the technical project manager to define workflow for the business and IT, and coordinated with Marketing and QA to define the rollout strategy and testing plan. She met with the sponsor and key stakeholders to review progress and make adjustments.

Everyone appeared satisfied with the direction of the project and the work completed to date. The excitement and enthusiasm grew with Anvi and her team as they saw their project moving from possibility to reality.

With each iteration and prototype test, their "gut reaction" was validated. They all could see the power of their collective knowledge and experience in play. It was an exciting time with emotions running high.

COMPLETE BUY-IN

This is the dream situation for a project manager or team leader - it is when the team is in synch, excited, and feeling empowered. Energy and enthusiasm are running high; heads and hearts of the stakeholders are engaged.

While we want that, the old cliché of "the higher they are, the harder they fall" comes to mind. In other words, bad news for a team like this can make or break it.

The tipping point for this is the way you assess, frame, and share it. That is what we will explore with the SED Method: Separate, Evaluate, and Deliver.

SEPARATE TO GAIN PERSPECTIVE

Change allows organizations to reinvent themselves, move in new directions, and recover from misfortune. In the project trenches, however, change may be viewed as a disturbance to our way of seeing and doing things.

Stakeholder tolerance for change varies but when we can envision and communicate the possibilities of the big picture while managing the emotions that surround the upheaval of change, the chances of moving successfully

| 60 |

Delivering Bad News in Good Ways:
Turn difficult conversations into purposeful dialogue, positive outcomes, & focused results in 3 easy steps

through the change process increase.

So, how do you (and your project team members) view change?

- ▷ Interruption to stability or the start of a journey
- ▷ Response to a disturbance or a path to innovation
- ▷ Problem or opportunity

If you said, "It depends," that would be a more than fair response because it does! If it did not then we would not need this or any other book, training session, lecture, or coaching on the subject.

Bad news typically invokes some kind of change. Large or small, change of any size makes an impact. And guess who is on the hook for facilitating? Yep, that would be you.

Thriving on change is fundamental to success as a project manager. Understanding the nature of change allows us to work with it instead of against it. Appreciating the conscious and unconscious emotional commitment of stakeholders provides clarity for how to manage it.

This begins with managers of projects and workflow, as Anvi discovers:

Everything seemed to be going well, but Anvi began to experience a nagging feeling growing in the pit of her stomach. Something was off. The sponsor, originally very enthusiastic about the project, seemed to be pulling back from it.

Initially, the change was barely noticeable, but over several months it became obvious the sponsor was growing increasingly unhappy. Finally during one of their weekly updates, Anvi asked the sponsor if there was a problem.

The sponsor suddenly blurted out she did not think the product approach was right, and she thought they should "go back to back to the drawing board and start over."

Anvi was crushed. One year's worth of intense research, design concept development, testing, and multiple rounds of vetting followed by several months of technical design and system development that were suddenly flushed down the drain.

Delivering Bad News in Good Ways:
Turn difficult conversations into purposeful dialogue, positive outcomes, & focused results in 3 easy steps

| 61 |

Countless hours of time and emotional investment were out the window. The thought of breaking the news to the team made Anvi feel sick to her stomach. She had to get a handle on her feelings before telling them.

Anvi noticed something critical in this situation: Once the impact of the news has settles in your mind (and body but more about that in Chapter 5), it is time to sort through it.

SEPARATE: BEGIN WITH YOURSELF

Before you can take on the emotional state of others, it is critical to get a handle on yourself first. It is with this frame of mind that you can assess and respond appropriately while also being more present with others.

To sort through your thoughts and feelings does not require taking up residence on a therapist's couch, but it does involve a time out like Anvi does in this next installment of her story.

Few had more of an emotional investment in the digital product development project than Anvi. As the product designer, she'd been with it since the concept stage and had never worked harder or longer on something as she did this project.

With that thought, she grabbed her mountain bike and took off for one of the longest trail rides of her life. As a competitive cyclist, this was a natural response. This activity always gave her the time she needed to chew through her thoughts and feelings about a situation and decide next steps.

Anvi dreaded breaking the news to the team, an automatic red flag that she needed to sort out her own feelings before tackling theirs.

Before jumping into a conversation about the bad news, it is important to understand what it means to you.

► What is your immediate emotional response?

► What impulse do you have?

► Are you scared or excited?

► Do you want to avoid it or promote it?

| 62 |

Delivering Bad News in Good Ways:
Turn difficult conversations into purposeful dialogue, positive outcomes, & focused results in 3 easy steps

▷ Does yelling and screaming at someone appeal to you or do you want to host a meeting that's like a pep rally?

▷ Do you just jump in and act without assessing your thoughts/feelings or do you give yourself time to collect and organize before acting?

▷ What change has your body experienced in response -- sweaty palms, stomach turns, heat in your chest?

Whatever immediate reaction you have, this is your amygdala talking to you. The hippocampus, reportedly the seat of memory, and the amygdala, the memory processor and emotions regulator, tag team to form your emotional response to anything you experience.

Whether you consciously realize it or not, for the most part we have feelings and thoughts about any experience, but the awareness of that is based on our brain's assessment of the situation courtesy of the cortex, the second-string events assessor that is much like the instant replay in sports.

The amygdala prepares the body for action and the cortex helps determine what players to put in the game. The amygdala and the cortex stay in touch with each other during the experience, but unfortunately the connection from the amygdala to the cortex is stronger than the cortex to the amygdala, which means too many players might be put in the game than is necessary.

This results in a potential overreaction in a given situation because of memories from some past event, as Doug Holt notes in his article *The Role of the Amygdala in Fear and Panic.*

Physical and emotional response is the first thing that surfaces for us in the face of bad news. Actually, we typically feel it before we are consciously aware of it.

This is what we will get into more deeply in Chapter 5, which goes into detail about what to do in the face of our own emotions and the emotions of others. It will also look at the importance of parsing fact from opinion so we can evaluate what needs done next.

Delivering Bad News in Good Ways:
Turn difficult conversations into purposeful dialogue, positive outcomes, & focused results in 3 easy steps

| 63 |

EVALUATE: UNDERSTAND YOUR OPTIONS AND NEEDS

In the face of bad news it is tempting to react, but as we see in Anvi's case, she hit the pause button to give her mind a chance to catch up with the boil in her body that resulted from the cancellation of her project. This pause gives her a chance to acknowledge her emotions so she could get on with the business of evaluating the situation.

Anvi took a very long bike ride to reflect on the sponsor's words that killed the project:

"IT JUST DOESN'T FEEL RIGHT."

As she picked up her pace she felt the heat of anger take hold. "It just doesn't feel right. Really? What is that supposed to mean?" The voice in her head yelled. "All that time, money, and effort wasted. People invested so much of themselves into this. That's a ridiculously inadequate reason. It's demoralizing and disrespectful."

The anger she felt lasted for most of the ride. By the time she finished, its energy had evaporated, and she began to wrap her head around what the change meant. Most of the work they'd done would be scrapped, so she considered how to talk to the team about it.

Options took shape about how they could learn from and leverage the project experience. Half-baked ideas about next steps took root as she wrapped up her workout.

Putting her bike away, she paused. Anvi had always been the resilient sort, but she knew others didn't bounce back like that. She'd learned long ago that people had to run their own cycle.

She was farther along in accepting the change, and had been able to work through it. Anvi knew she would have to assume a facilitation and support role when she broke the news so they'd have time to be with as she had done. Patience. That's what her team needed from her.

| 64 |

Delivering Bad News in Good Ways:
Turn difficult conversations into purposeful dialogue, positive outcomes, & focused results in 3 easy steps

SIMPLE CHANGE PROCESS

Understanding the stages of change is essential to managing change effectively among those with whom we work and within ourselves.

There are many models to describe the stages of change, but most follow a pattern similar to this one I teach in *Systemation's* workshop called *Maximizing Project Success through People:*

Chaos. First stage. Emotions may or may not be strong, running a broad spectrum of responses from positive to negative. Common emotions include denial, anger, and confusion.

Clarity. Change involves uncertainty about the future so it is rarely communicated as a complete, cohesive idea. Initiators of change often do not fully understand all aspects of the direction that they wish to go. During the clarity stage people start to deal with what the change means.

Creativity. In this stage, stakeholders begin to establish a clear understanding of the change and begin thinking about ideas for instituting or operationalizing it. It is here that people can start facing the challenges of the new reality.

Continuity. This is the transition from turbulence to stability and a new way of working. New procedures are established for operating. The process of "tweaking" the new reality begins.

This change model does not follow a particular order. All steps must be experienced and people may revisit one or more of them. You also cannot force a person or team through the steps. It is an individual experience.

The SED Method supports the change process. It gives us a way to manage ourselves, anticipate the thoughts and feelings of others, and problem solve through the change process. It is the delivery process that rounds out the SED Method.

Delivering Bad News in Good Ways:
Turn difficult conversations into purposeful dialogue, positive outcomes, & focused results in 3 easy steps

| 65 |

DELIVER: APPLY THE RESULTS OF YOUR ASSESSMENT

This is the opportunity to leverage your assessment of the situation and share your options, which opens the door to dialogue that leads (hopefully) to negotiation and collaboration.

In preparation to tell the team about the canceled project, Anvi identified possible emotional reactions, evaluated options, and determined the best way to approach her team given the circumstances. The delivery step was critical to helping her team recover from the "chaos" of the change and refocus.

Let's see how Anvi does this.

Anvi took a deep breath before she addressed the angry project team. A few minutes earlier the hastily assembled meeting was full of buzz until the sponsor and Anvi entered the room.

The sponsor looked at them without any emotion as she told the team that the product development project they had devoted a year to had been killed. The reasoning the sponsor gave them was nothing more than what she'd said to Anvi the day before: "It just doesn't feel right."

The sponsor promptly turned and walked out. Anvi was left to deal with the fallout. She opened her mouth to tell them her carefully thought through plan for their next steps, but she didn't get chance. The room erupted with emotion, which wasn't really a surprise to her. She waited and listened.

"What is she doing?" One person said. "Is she crazy? We killed ourselves on that thing," another team member said. The protests went on for several minutes and then Anvi stepped in.

"All of us are shocked by this turn of events," she said, "and we all feel there should be more reason than what was provided. But there's not and we don't have any control over that. We do have control over our response to it."

Anvi paused. Her eyes scanned the room. A variety of expressions on their faces told her most were not really listening to her.

"Okay, look," Anvi calmly said. "We're not going to get anywhere today. Let's take a break and reconvene when we've had a chance to let this sink in.

| 66 |

Delivering Bad News in Good Ways:
Turn difficult conversations into purposeful dialogue, positive outcomes, & focused results in 3 easy steps

Come back tomorrow ready to focus how we can leverage what we learned on the project so we can go back to the drawing board. We WILL learn from it. We WILL develop the product. We WILL give our customers the best product possible."

No one moved initially, but slowly they stirred and shuffled out. Anvi knew she had a star team but also knew they were human and needed some time to absorb the new reality.

SUCCESSFULLY MANAGING CHANGE STARTS WITH YOU.

Understanding your tolerance for change will give you a chance to recognize symptoms inside you for when your tolerance has been reached. Team emotions tend to reflect that of the leader, and if the leader is stressed, then the team probably will be as well.

To improve your ability to recognize and manage change, consider the following:

- ▶ Do the emotional work first

- ▶ Plan

- ▶ Be aware of which stage you are in

- ▶ Be aware of the stage people are in

- ▶ Communicate early and often

Delivering Bad News in Good Ways:
Turn difficult conversations into purposeful dialogue, positive outcomes, & focused results in 3 easy steps

| 67 |

In the following chapters, we will explore in more detail how you can do this with confidence and support using the steps of the SED Method.

CHAPTER TAKEAWAYS

▶ Overview of the SED Model

▶ Simple application of SED to support the overview

▶ Challenges faced with evolving technology

▶ Awareness of emotions

▶ Change process

| 68 |

Delivering Bad News in Good Ways:
Turn difficult conversations into purposeful dialogue, positive outcomes, & focused results in 3 easy steps

CHAPTER 5:

SEPARATE STEP OF THE SED METHOD

GET THE FACTS STRAIGHT FIRST

FREE, OPEN MEETING PLACE TAKES A BLOW

It was humid, sticky evening in Atlanta, Georgia. Despite the swelter of the hottest month there that year, thousands of people packed Centennial Olympic Park to hear Jack Mack and the Heart Attack. It was July 27, eight days into the 1996 Summer Olympic Games, and to that point there had been few reported incidents.

The Atlanta Committee for the Olympic Games, law enforcement, and military personnel had spent several years preparing for the Games of the XXVI Olympiad and the Paralympics that followed.

Security at more than thirty event venues across the state was tight. Two to three checkpoints with metal detectors at many locations provided layers of security needed to help the public feel secure.

This was deemed necessary in the recent wake of the Trans World Airlines Boeing 747 bound for Paris that exploded after leaving New York, killing all 230 people on board.

During the many intense security planning sessions before the games started, strategy and response details were repeatedly created and practiced. Careful consideration was given when assessing the number of security personnel that would be visible at each location.

I know. I was there and co-facilitated several of those sessions.

While the security numbers were heavy at almost all the venues, there was one venue where it was limited: Centennial Olympic Park. It was feared that having too many uniformed security personnel would scare the public. Olympic officials wanted the park to be a "free and open meeting place for the world."

Around 1 a.m. as fans enjoyed the music, security guard Richard Jewell discovered a backpack, which was stuffed with three pipe bombs surrounded by three-inch-long masonry nails. As he and other security personnel worked to clear the area, the bomb detonated at 1:25 a.m.

| 70 |

Delivering Bad News in Good Ways:
Turn difficult conversations into purposeful dialogue, positive outcomes, & focused results in 3 easy steps

Two people died that night, one directly from the blast and the other from a heart attack, and 111 were wounded. It shut the park for a few days while investigators worked.

Shortly after the bomb detonated, military personnel were alerted to increase uniformed presence at the park. In response, facts were gathered to understand what happened, the impact, and the actions that followed the bombing.

The fact-gathering step was critical to evaluating the number of people needed, how long they would be needed, and what gear they would need to have on hand during their shifts.

It was also important to assess who was going to do what, particularly when it came to managing public response to uniformed personnel presence.

Delivering Bad News in Good Ways:
Turn difficult conversations into purposeful dialogue, positive outcomes, & focused results in 3 easy steps

| 71 |

SEPARATE: HOW YOU DO IT

The events on the night of July 27 and the activities that followed provided insight into how civilian and military officials carefully gathered facts to ensure they could respond to the request to add more uniformed personnel to the park venue. But it is not just in crisis and disaster work where fact gathering is critical.

Consider the following business examples:

Your project sponsor has significantly reduced your funding but still expects the same scope.

A major issue discovered during testing will require an additional three months work, which will impact the critical due date. Oh, and by the way, in anticipation that the project would wrap up on time, you've already started ramping up management of a new and even larger project!

Two primary project stakeholders can't seem to agree on a solution for a crucial part of system build. The situation has eroded quickly and now they are refusing to work together.

As we considered in Chapter 4, change is a reality on projects. I have always said I would love for a plan to be etched in stone right out of the gate, but we all know that is not possible. There are simply too many variables and unknowns, so we lay out the plan to the best of our ability and then respond and make adjustments with new information along the way.

The management part of this is using processes to **collect, integrate,** and **distribute** information and work requirements to stakeholders. There are many fine publications that provide guidance and details for how to manage these processes.

What is not necessarily covered in equivalent detail in other books is how to **assess, respond,** and **manage** the emotional experience of change on the stakeholders (and you).

Because bad news is often the result of a change, we will break down the parts of the SED Method to help with assessing, responding, and managing the emotional experience of it.

| 72 |

Delivering Bad News in Good Ways:
Turn difficult conversations into purposeful dialogue, positive outcomes, & focused results in 3 easy steps

STEP 1 OF SEPARATE: DEFINE THE SITUATION/EVENT

Bad news is on the table: Now what?

Alexander Pope (1688-1744) said, "To err is human; to forgive, divine."

For the sake of managing projects and workflow, let's give it a new spin:

To err is human; to separate and sort before responding, divine.

When change is needed, it is natural to jump right into a bunch of assumptions. It is even more natural to make one of those assumptions your conclusion before you have fully assessed the situation.

This is just the way the mind works — we use **mental models** to quickly assess and respond to the situation at hand.

As we established in the previous chapter, our mind is constantly sifting through tons of information in an effort to make sense of the environment and experiences around us.

The human brain likes order and will work very hard to create it as soon as possible in an effort to quickly resume stasis. It is important to understand the following:

"Context is the reality of the situation around us. Without context, our minds have a tendency to take shortcuts & recognize patterns that aren't really there. We connect the dots without first collecting the dots." From the book **The Mission, the Men, and Me** *by Pete Blaber*

The upside of this is it enables us to respond rapidly to a variety of situations, to innovate, and to create. The downside is we make a ton of assumptions that miss the mark.

As a matter of fact, research shows 40 to 50 percent of the time our assumptions are correct, but here is the rub: 50 to 60 percent of the time those assumptions are NOT correct.

Hmmm...time for a reality check, you say? Yep, you are a quick one.

Let's take a look at how that process works.

Delivering Bad News in Good Ways:
Turn difficult conversations into purposeful dialogue, positive outcomes, & focused results in 3 easy steps

| 73 |

MAKING SENSE OF INFORMATION

Maybe you're standing around the airport gate waiting to board your plane and an interesting person catches your eye.

Perhaps you've just been named manager of a project that's been in progress for several months. You steal a quick glance at the team before getting down to business.

You're at a networking event and you see someone who looks like a person you met before. You walk up to say hello, but then you suddenly realize this isn't the same person.

What's happening in your head during the initial moment of those situations? In what seems like an *instant,* thoughts creep into your consciousness. You might *reflexively* make a statement about the person in your head, and then counter that thought with an "Oh, where did THAT impression come from?"

Possibly you simply react without any forethought. Hopefully, there is no fallout from that potential *"uh-oh"* moment, which is when you act on the thought without thinking about it and it does not turn out well.

So, how long do you think an *instant* is if you timed it? Perhaps you are thinking it is only a few minutes or several seconds.

What is going on with your *reflexive* response? Maybe your response is that you "just know" or it's "intuition."

How can you form an *impression* of someone else so quickly? Where does it come from? Perhaps you simply assume that being on the planet and having a variety of experiences just gives you license to make quick decisions and conclusions without vetting them.

If any of those responses rolled through your head you're not far off, but as with most things, there is a process we naturally follow.

Here is one process that can help understand it.

| 74 |

Delivering Bad News in Good Ways:
Turn difficult conversations into purposeful dialogue, positive outcomes, & focused results in 3 easy steps

MAGIC OF YOUR MIND: THE THINKING (AND FEELING) PROCESS EXPLAINED

Many years ago, I was curious about how our minds could react so instantly to people and things around us. At the time, it seemed to me impressions and thoughts came out of nowhere like magic, but I knew that did not make sense.

I started researching to understand the process. My hunch was that if we better understood this seemingly **magical** process, we might have an opportunity to respond more thoughtfully and intentionally when communicating with and responding to others.

So, how long *does* it take to form an impression of someone?

Well, based on a series of experiments by psychologists Janine Willis and Alexander Todorov, it takes around a *100 milliseconds*. To give you a sense of just how brief that is, let's use an example from language.

All languages have phonemes, which are sounds unique within that language. In English, we have the phoneme "cha," which takes about 250 milliseconds to say.

Yep, that's fast, but *how is it possible that an impression can pop up so quickly?*

BREAKING DOWN THE MAGIC

The brain has three major parts – the brainstem, the limbic area, and the cortical area. The brainstem is the oldest part of our brains, and it is the bit we share with the lower-ordered creatures on the planet like snakes and other reptiles.

Delivering Bad News in Good Ways:
Turn difficult conversations into purposeful dialogue, positive outcomes, & focused results in 3 easy steps

| 75 |

This is the part of the brain that takes care of autonomic functions like breathing, digestive processing, eliminating waste, and other bodily activities.

The brainstem regulates all those functions and keeps them in check, which simply means we do not have to chew up our awareness with saying, "Come on, heart, pump," or "Breathe, lungs, breathe..." although you might feel that way when climbing that last set of stairs or running/cycling that last mile!

The limbic brain is what one of my children affectionately refers to as the "feeling" brain. This section is the seat of our memories.

When events occur, it is this part of the brain that tells our mind and body how to feel in response. So when we encounter a long lost friend, see a tear-jerking video ad on television or social media, or hear someone crying or screaming, it is this part of our brain that calls up a memory which then triggers the chemicals inside of us that floods our body with an emotional response.

The cortical brain is the newest part of our brain, and it is considered our "thinking" brain. This is the part that uses logic to sort information and give it some order.

It allows us to assess what we are experiencing in our environment and then respond, which is critical to survival because it gives us the pause we need to assess carefully how to respond to an event.

The rub here is that the thinking brain is **slower** than the limbic brain. Remember the *100 milliseconds* it takes for our brains to come up with an impression? Well, the limbic brain is quick on the trigger.

The cortical brain, on the other hand, needs a bit more time - about *3.6 seconds* to be exact.

I think you know where I'm going with this...

| 76 |

Delivering Bad News in Good Ways:
Turn difficult conversations into purposeful dialogue, positive outcomes, & focused results in 3 easy steps

BRIDGING THE GAP BETWEEN 100 MILLISECONDS AND 3.6 SECONDS

Just like most things in life, there is a process and the first impression response is no exception. There is a lot of science to this process, but to keep it simple, I have clustered the thinking/feeling process into three groups:

1. Collect
2. Filter
3. Respond

What is interesting about the process is how it develops based on your experiences. What is even more interesting? It is not a one-time thing – it's not fixed. The brain reorganizes and forms neural connections, which means it can grow, change, and evolve over your lifetime.

Neuroscientists call it neuroplasticity. Your professional and personal experiences, the people in your life, the things you do all inform this process.

What does that mean to you and someone with whom you are working?

When you sit down to have a conversation with that person, you might think you and the other person are the only two people there, but actually that is not the case.

The reality is you BOTH bring loads of people and experiences into the conversation. It's not two people – **it's a party!** As a matter of fact, it is the "party" we bring with us into conversations that inspired the selection of the image at the beginning of the chapter.

It is these past experiences that help you make sense of the current experience.

If your experience is limited or very different from the person with whom you are communicating, well, then things can get mighty complicated really fast.

Let's see how that plays out...

Delivering Bad News in Good Ways:
Turn difficult conversations into purposeful dialogue, positive outcomes, & focused results in 3 easy steps

| 77 |

1: COLLECT: HOW WE TAKE IN INFORMATION

As we noted in Chapter 4, we sort and sift through tons information every second of every day through a variety of sources.

► COLLECT: INFORMATION CONSUMPTION

This is how we receive information.

- ► Visual
- ► Auditory
- ► Memory
- ► Language
- ► Mental Imagery
- ► Skin
- ► Emotions
- ► Internal Cues

We take information in through our eyes, nose, mouth, skin, and ears. We also respond to internal functions and cycles unique to each of us. For example, hormone levels in women and men vary to some degree each month, as we will consider later in this chapter.

Neuroscience research has shown that our brains can grow whole new neural networks based on what we pay attention to and practice. As mentioned in the previous section, this is called neuroplasticity.

Basically, neuroplasticity supports the idea that we can teach an old dog new tricks, so to speak, and what we pay attention to shapes aspects of our thinking and feeling brains. As a result, we respond to internal cues associated with what we tend to pay attention to in our environment.

| 78 |

Delivering Bad News in Good Ways:
Turn difficult conversations into purposeful dialogue, positive outcomes, & focused results in 3 easy steps

2: FILTER: SEPARATE THE WHEAT FROM THE CHAFF

We cannot possibly actively acknowledge the 11 trillion bits of information, as mentioned in Chapter 4, so our mind has designed a very unique filtering system to allow us to pay attention to certain information.

And when I say "unique," I mean unique to you as an individual. What is not necessarily unique are the sources that help you filter that information, as illustrated in the graphic below.

▶ FILTER: COGNITIVE COMPRESSION

This is how we sort and make sense of the information.

- ▷ Experiences
- ▷ Events
- ▷ Family
- ▷ Friends
- ▷ Education
- ▷ Interest
- ▷ Religion
- ▷ Culture
- ▷ Ethnicity
- ▷ Values/Beliefs
- ▷ Past
- ▷ Current State
- ▷ Knowledge

Delivering Bad News in Good Ways:
Turn difficult conversations into purposeful dialogue, positive outcomes, & focused results in 3 easy steps

| 79 |

To filter is to do something psychologist call cognitive compression, but more about that in just a bit. Let's use an example first.

Most of us had the experience when we had to read something several times or ask someone to restate what they have said once or twice before it started to make sense. Maybe you even doodled about what you just read or what you chatted about with a friend.

When we encounter something new to us, it is fair to say that we are probably not going to "get it" right off the bat. Some things need a bit more time to sift through to have them sink in – to take root in our minds.

So, you run through some questions in your head. You might compare the current information to past experience. Questions you may ask:

- What have I experienced in the past that is most like what is in front of me now?

- How did I handle it?

- Whom do I know who has dealt with this subject before?

- What did they do to address it?

- What worked about their approach? What did not work?

- How do I feel about this?

It is questions like these that we naturally run through when faced with a new situation. In certain situations we just seem to "know" what to do. Experience and "muscle memory" are often in play in that case. This is when you know something so well you do not have to think about it.

The process, however, slows down when we are not as familiar with the content. This is when we draw on the broader set of our experience, values, culture, and beliefs to determine how to respond to a particular situation.

When we filter we are using a process called **cognitive compression.** Once upon a time, scientists thought the brain acted much like a recorder. In our more enlightened age we now know that the brain tends to categorize information.

| 80 |

Delivering Bad News in Good Ways:
Turn difficult conversations into purposeful dialogue, positive outcomes, & focused results in 3 easy steps

Cognitive compression helps us categorize the world and reduce the convolution of conceptual structures to a more manageable scale.

It allows the brain to reduce the complexity and ease understanding by chunking it. It also helps the brain to recall the information more quickly, but not always more accurately.

While this is very efficient, the potential also exists to oversimplify a situation or concept. A classic example of this is Einstein's theory of relativity. To help us mere mortals grasp the concept, over time the phrase "Everything is relative" was coined.

There is a warning in that example. The mind does not tolerate ambiguity or confusion very well or for long. In an effort to reduce any anxiety or stress that might result, our mind has a tendency to filter through associations quickly.

This fast filtering can lead us down the wrong path. There is some science to this, which we will cover in Chapter 6 when we review Daniel Kahneman and Amos Tversky System 1 and System 2 framework.

3: RESPOND: INTERACTION BASED ON INTERPRETATION
RESPOND: PERCEPTION & UNDERSTANDING

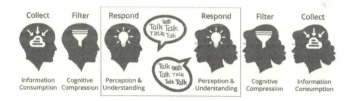

Our response based on what we pay attention to and how we interpret it. This is usually a combination of the following, which we may or may not be fully aware of in the moment: Thoughts & Feelings.

Collect and Filter shape our Thoughts and Feelings. This is what informs our perception and understand and influences how we talk to each other.

So, do we use short cuts to respond? Why, yes! And we mentioned them earlier - they are called mental models. Now it is time to take a closer look...

Delivering Bad News in Good Ways:
Turn difficult conversations into purposeful dialogue, positive outcomes, & focused results in 3 easy steps

| 81 |

MINDING YOUR MENTAL MODELS

While the mind is extremely efficient with sorting through volumes of information to quickly gain the understanding needed to respond to a given situation, it is also the same structure that can lead us down a very wrong path.

Consider the characteristics of the mental model structure:

► Sometimes is based on incomplete facts, obscure ideas, and difficult to quantify information

► Can be flexible or rigid based on individual experience and focus

► Tends to create selective attention - we usually pay attention to the most familiar

"JUST THE FACTS, MA'AM"

So, how do we pull back from rolling down the wrong path loaded with a backpack of assumptions? Take a deep breath and let your "thinking" brain step in and go to work.

Although dated, the quote above is very appropriate. "Just the facts, ma'am" became a catchphrase for a 1960s TV crime drama series that found its beginnings in a radio show that ran from 1949 to 1957. Sgt. Joe Friday used the phrase when interviewing witnesses to help them separate fact from opinion.

In the spirit of Joe Friday, that is what you as a project manager are initially tasked to do when you first learn of potential bad news. Separating fact from opinion is not easy, as we learned when we considered the Thinking Process in the previous section. Because of unique experiences, some people will label news as "bad" while others will be more casual about it.

The objective here is not to ignore feelings about a situation but rather to manage them so you can ACT instead of REACT. The ACT/REACT dynamic has roots in cognitive theory, a branch of psychology. It goes something like this:

| 82 |

Delivering Bad News in Good Ways:
Turn difficult conversations into purposeful dialogue, positive outcomes, & focused results in 3 easy steps

EVENT + RESPONSE = REACT

Let's say you are driving down the road and another driver cuts you off. What do you do? Perhaps you will have a few colorful words and direct some choice hand signals at the offending driver. This is an example where you see an event and simply react in accordance with whatever bubbles up to your awareness.

In crisis situations, this is not a bad thing. Muscle memory gets flexed in a crisis response and gives you what you need to respond quickly because the situation is potentially life threatening.

In non-threatening situations, however, this approach will likely lead to "uh-oh" moments where you act before you think or you draw an incorrect conclusion. To avoid "uh-oh" moments or solving the wrong problem, it is more effective to do the following:

EVENT + ASSESS + SELECT = ACT

Adding one extra step can go a long way to responding to the situation in a more appropriate way. Let's take the driving example again, but add this new step.

You are driving down the road and another driver cuts you off. Saying a few colorful words and directing some choice hand signals at the offending driver will still likely surface, but instead immediately doing them, your thinking brain throws some possibilities into your head:

▶ Maybe the person did not see me

▶ Perhaps they just received an urgent phone call and they have to rush to the hospital

▶ It is possible that...

By the time you get to the third possibility, the initial emotion you experienced with seeing the breach of driving protocol has passed. Basically, you have moved on AND you have avoided an emotional hijacking where you react instead of act.

Delivering Bad News in Good Ways:
Turn difficult conversations into purposeful dialogue, positive outcomes, & focused results in 3 easy steps

| 83 |

When we react in response to our initial emotions about something, we are, in a sense, giving our emotions over to someone else. It is these moments where we risk saying things we can never take back or doing things we cannot reverse.

By pausing to assess, we give our thinking brain a chance to catch up (remember, it needs 3.6 seconds). This reminds me of my mother.

When I was a kid and she was unhappy with something I did, she would count to 10. In my child brain, I assumed it was a countdown to punishment.

As an adult and parent, I can now appreciate what she was doing. Counting to 10 gave her thinking brain a chance to catch up with her emotional brain so she could respond thoughtfully, mindfully instead of giving in to an "uh-oh" moment.

Moms are pretty smart.

| 84 |

Delivering Bad News in Good Ways:
Turn difficult conversations into purposeful dialogue, positive outcomes, & focused results in 3 easy steps

CREATING A PAUSE TO ASSESS

Building in a pause to assess "bad" news before responding is something you probably already do in some situations. Let's say, for example, you are about to deliver an important presentation. When you turn on your computer, nothing happens. Initially, you might feel surge of frustration or panic, but then you step back mentally and roll through a series of questions:

▶ Is it plugged in?

▶ Is the battery charged?

▶ Does it need to be rebooted?

▶ Did I bring the flash drive with the extra copy?

While your feeling brain is ready to spring into action, your thinking brain slows the process by asking questions that deepen understanding so you can manage and respond in the best way.

Years ago, I learned about a method that is similar to this process. Called ORID, it is a facilitated method created by the *Institute for Cultural* Affairs to enable teams to analyze facts, assess feelings, understand implications, and make thoughtful decisions about a past, present, or future event. Here is the ORID breakdown:

Objective discussion: Draws out the facts about the event so the group can gain a deeper understanding of the situation.

Reflective discussion: Facilitates group discussion regarding how team members feel or felt about the event.

Interpretive discussion: Helps the participants assess the meaning, significance, and value relative to their operational or project objectives.

Decisional discussion: Moves the participants into a decision or response position that enables them to respond appropriately to the situation.

For the purpose of the pause, in this next section we will consider how to adapt the ORID method to create the pause needed for the Separate step of the SED method for delivering bad news in good ways.

We will look at *Objective, Reflective, and Interpretative* as a series of **questions** we ask ourselves or use when working/problem solving with others.

Delivering Bad News in Good Ways:
Turn difficult conversations into purposeful dialogue, positive outcomes, & focused results in 3 easy steps

| 85 |

ASKING THE RIGHT QUESTIONS AT THE RIGHT TIME

Many years ago, my then five-year old daughter was in quite a state when I picked her up from Montessori school. At a speed I hardly thought capable of her, words rushed, bumped, and swirled as she bounced around the details of an event that occurred earlier in the day.

As she struggled to relay non-sequential thoughts and feelings, her voice progressively filled with tears of frustration and anger while vacillating in speed and intonation.

Concerned and confused, I asked her to slow down because I needed to catch up. I explained to her that while she had been with this situation for most of the day, I was just hearing it for the first time, so it was new for me.

Relief spread across her face as I eased her through a series of questions. I explained to her that I needed to ask these questions before I could jump in and share her feelings.

It took a little time and a lot of patience, but eventually we mapped out the facts of the event. Ironically, walking through the facts helped my daughter decide that the situation was not as bad as she first thought.

She also was able to see the role she played in the sequence of events. With tears dried and calm fully settled in her little frame, unbeknownst to her we finished the ORID questions, and she left the conversation feeling better about her next steps.

Although it is a personal example, the process can be applied across a variety of subjects. What I did with my daughter was to ask Objective Questions.

| 86 |

Delivering Bad News in Good Ways:
Turn difficult conversations into purposeful dialogue, positive outcomes, & focused results in 3 easy steps

OBJECTIVE QUESTIONS: JUST THE FACTS

Taking a few minutes to ask questions is one aspect of what is called Active Listening. Active Listening involves three main components:

Be present: Stop other activity and pay attention to what the other person is saying

Probe: Ask questions to deepen understanding

Paraphrase: Take what the other person said and confirm your understanding by restating it in your own words

Whether face-to-face or virtual, these three simple activities help you focus the discussion and better understand what is needed from you. It also helps you establish trust with the other person. That person will slow down and relax if they think you really understand what they are sharing.

Trust creates goodwill and both parties will feel more inclined to partner and work through the situation when they both feel trust is present, but it has to start somewhere.

Since you can only control you, then you are in the best position to make the first move in the trust department, and that starts with asking questions.

Often when a person is recounting the events of a situation, they mix facts with opinion. It is the mixing that can make it challenging to follow the story.

When the person is feeling emotionally charged from the event, they not only mix fact with opinion, they tell the story out of sequence and at an accelerated pace which makes it even MORE difficult to understand.

Oh, and by the way, the other person is not the only person who does this. You do it, too. We all do!

Delivering Bad News in Good Ways:
Turn difficult conversations into purposeful dialogue, positive outcomes, & focused results in 3 easy steps

| 87 |

ESTABLISHING CONTEXT BEFORE DIVING INTO OBJECTIVE Qs

When you ask Objective Questions, it gives you a chance to establish the facts in the situation, influence the pace of the discussion, and manage the flow of information. It also gives you context so you can better understand how to respond. A good way to kick off your questions is to give them context for what you are about to do.

For example, you could say the following:

"Okay, there's a fair amount of information here. I need to ask a few questions to understand all of it before I can weigh in."

"I wonder if you could humor me by answering a few questions. I am not sure I understand it as well as you, but I am sure your answers will bring me a lot closer."

"Wow, there's a lot going on in this story that is really interesting. Let me ask you a few questions to make sure I am tracking with you."

IN OBJECTIVE QUESTIONS, DESIGN MATTERS

Consider the two questions:

How's your morning going?

versus

What kind of response did you get from the team this morning about the idea you pitched for the project?

The first question is obviously very general. A simple "Good" is a sufficient response, but very little information is really shared. The second question is more specific and will likely yield more details that can create an opportunity to go deeper with the subject.

Of course, the way you craft your question is dependent on its purpose. You may want a general, simple answer because you do not have time or are not inclined to jump into a conversation with the other person. If, however, you

| 88 |

Delivering Bad News in Good Ways:
Turn difficult conversations into purposeful dialogue, positive outcomes, & focused results in 3 easy steps

need or want to go deeper, a more specific question is needed. Ask for what you want.

A more specific question is also needed for context. When seeking information from someone, you are actually playing the dual role of **investigator** and **facilitator.** The key to this dual role is question design.

It is just as important as the answers received and this starts with crafting questions with an eye to how the brain works. Neuroscience is beginning to give us deep insight into how our brains work.

Here are a few things to keep in mind as you move through the Separate step:

▶ Explaining what we see in our heads in a way that makes sense to others is difficult because our respective experiences and assumptions are so different from others

▶ We know we cannot remember in exact detail the events that occurred in the past

▶ Our mind CHANGES memory details over time

▶ The more we practice something the more intuitive it becomes

▶ The more familiar we are with something, the harder it becomes for us to explain it

Let's take a deeper look and consider what we can say and do to compensate when asking Objective Questions.

Delivering Bad News in Good Ways:
Turn difficult conversations into purposeful dialogue, positive outcomes, & focused results in 3 easy steps

| 89 |

CREATING A CANVAS WITH OBJECTIVE Q WORDS

*"Si dipinge col cervello et non con le mani," which means "One paints with
the brain and not the hands." ~ Michelangelo Buonarotti*

With our understanding today of how the brain works, no truer words were
ever spoken. Michelangelo understood well that creativity starts in the mind,
but a person sometimes needs some help transferring a vision or concept
into their medium of choice.

This is why artists, writers, sculptors, and designers will take time to visit
museums, study, travel to new places, and read material of all sorts.

It not only gives them ideas to deepen and refine the concept, it gives
them the language they need to share those ideas so the larger group can
understand.

This, in part, is what I think separates good from great in art, writing, and other
creative endeavors – the "language" of the creative piece is universal to the
point that we know it and recognize it without really understanding how or why.
It is this "language" that is the key to the rest of us connecting with it.

What does this have to do with Objective Questions? Let's look at a situation
that illustrates the importance of the words we use when asking them.

*Taking a break from having her head deep in a design step for a new
website application, Jamie stole a quick glance at her mobile phone and
saw that Samir, one of her design partners, had called five times.*

*Although the voice messages were brief, it was clear he was really excited.
For months they had been trying to solve a very complex issue with a piece
of functionality, but so far nothing had worked.*

*Based on the tone in his voice, it sounded like he might have found
something that would solve the issue. After to listening to the fifth message,
Jamie found her excitement growing, too. So many late nights, the push
and pull of ideas, and discarded attempts had brought them close to the
brink of giving up on it. With a smile on her face, she pushed "call back" on
her phone.*

| 90 |

Delivering Bad News in Good Ways:
Turn difficult conversations into purposeful dialogue, positive outcomes, & focused results in 3 easy steps

"Holy cow, Jamie! What took you so long," Samir said in a too-loud voice.

"Sorry, mate...I went dark for a while to work out the user flow for the architect, otherwise I would have phoned you back straight away," she said with a sincere tone.

Samir didn't bother to respond but dove headlong into his idea to solve the issue. He took leaps around the idea like a kid jumping in a random pattern on a trampoline. Jamie tried her best to keep up, but it was impossible.

He bounced from how the idea could work to where he was when he got the idea to what the idea was similar to that he saw in the place he visited. She didn't want to crush his enthusiasm, but she wanted to make sure she understood what he was saying.

Samir was a genius artist and digital designer in every sense, who was always a few steps ahead of everyone else in just about everything. In addition to being a brilliant creative, he could also be as characteristically temperamental.

With careful consideration, she said, "Samir, this is so awesome – I really think you've hit on something important here. Just to make sure I'm following your train of thought, let me ask you a few questions.

"Shoot," he said eagerly.

Sensing that he wanted and needed to tell the story that led up to his radical idea and recognizing the story background would help her contribute to the idea, she kicked off her questions with asking for facts about how the idea came about.

She used "sensing" words to help create a picture in her mind that she hoped looked something like what Samir was thinking.

We have established that context is king when it comes to creating a deeper understanding of a situation. While not always needed, there is value in understanding the "backstory" of something. Backstory is a literary device used to provide the background behind a story, characters, a piece of art, and the like.

Delivering Bad News in Good Ways:
Turn difficult conversations into purposeful dialogue, positive outcomes, & focused results in 3 easy steps

| 91 |

The backstory can give insight into why and how the result came about. It can also be very helpful when evolving an idea with a team as part of the iteration process. Having insight into what the originator was thinking can fuel further ideas essential to the objective.

Jamie was on the right path with Samir. Although there was no particular order to his story, the fact that he chose to describe the place he was when he got the idea, what he saw while he was he was there, and how that got him on the path to the current idea gave Jamie the clue that her understanding of those things would be important to them when working together to evolve the idea.

She also understood showing some patience as he shared details would help him feel confident and trust that her objective was to move to a collaborative place. She likely kicked things off with sensing questions like the following:

- What did you see when you got there?

- How did it smell or what scent did it remind you of?

- What flavors did you taste?

- How did it feel to your touch?

- What did you hear? What did it sound like?

It is perfectly okay to follow up the questions with suggestions that reflect the sense you are using, particularly if the person seems at a loss for how to describe it.

For example, for the question about touch, you could follow up with, "Did it feel rough, smooth, bumpy, or soft?" For the question about sound, you could follow up with "Was it high pitched, low pitched, loud, or barely audible?"

You get the idea, but there is a caveat. It is important to give the person a chance to answer the question without prompting first. This will avoid "leading" the person to a direction of your choice or "putting words in their mouth," so to speak.

As stated earlier, we tend to feel things before we think and it works that way in our memories as well. As a result, using words that engage the senses

| 92 |

Delivering Bad News in Good Ways:
Turn difficult conversations into purposeful dialogue, positive outcomes, & focused results in 3 easy steps

can help us recall things regarding the situation. It also gives you, as the person facilitating, a deeper understanding of the experience and what it meant to them.

Taking what we see in our heads and explaining it in a way that makes sense to others is challenging, but it is not impossible to do.

Although our respective experiences and assumptions tend to be different from others, when we use sensing words when asking Objective Questions, we have a greater chance of finding a common understanding of the situation and supporting events.

Let's take a look at some techniques and considerations (and complications) to tease out the facts...

Delivering Bad News in Good Ways:
Turn difficult conversations into purposeful dialogue, positive outcomes, & focused results in 3 easy steps

| 93 |

TEASING OUT THE FACTS IN A LESS THAN EXACT WORLD

▶ MEMORY

While we might think our memory is solid (and even take pride in it!), we actually cannot remember in exact detail the events that occurred in the past. And in an even more remarkable twist, our minds can CHANGE the details over time.

As an example, the reliability rate of witnesses to a crime has been proven to be quite low. Marc Green, Ph.D., in his article, *Errors in Eyewitness Identification Procedure,* attributes the low reliability rate to a number of factors.

"Why is mistaken identity so common? One reason is poor encoding at time of initial perception. This could be due to poor visibility (bad lighting, brief duration, long distance, etc.) or to the tricks played by human perception. A second reason is faulty memory."

"Memory has several quirks which affect reliability, including 1) low resolution (a remembered face is not as clear as one actually viewed), 2) the tendency for memories to be constructed so that missing information is supplied from expectations/biases or from an external source (TV, newspaper, other witnesses, the police, etc.) or from other memories and 3) systematic perceptual distortions in memory (small sizes grow and large sizes shrink, colors are remembered as brighter, etc)."

David Brooks, author of **The Social Animal,** adds the following:

"When information gets stored in the brain, it doesn't just get filed away. It seems to get moved about...Memory doesn't actually retrieve information. It reweaves it. Things that happen later can transform your memory of something that happened before."

The unfortunate result is that our memories are not quite as reliable as we think they are. Examples:

▶ Challenger explosion. Ulric Neisser asked students to write down where and what they were doing at the time of the explosion. Two and a half years later a quarter of the respondents gave different accounts of their whereabouts during the explosion.

| 94 |

Delivering Bad News in Good Ways:
Turn difficult conversations into purposeful dialogue, positive outcomes, & focused results in 3 easy steps

- 77 percent of prisoners exonerated based on DNA evidence were convicted based on eyewitness accounts.

- Current feelings and mood can influence how we remember things

- Stereotypes can influence how we remember an event

- Our experience can influence how we hear another's account of an event.

- How we ask questions, our emotional affect can influence how someone responds to our questions

- Cultural variants can have us misinterpret facial expressions; e.g., in his publication, *Emotions Revealed, Paul Ekman,* noted psychologist and researcher of facial expressions, "I tested this formulation in a series of studies that showed that when alone Japanese and Americans displayed the same facial expressions in response to seeing films of surgery and accidents, but when a scientist sat with them as they watched the films, Japanese more than the Americans masked negative expressions with a smile. In private, innate expressions; in public, managed expressions."

- Tend to only remember the emotional climax of an event and the end.

▶ MUSCLE MEMORY

The more we practice something, the more intuitive it becomes. This is called muscle memory. While muscle memory is useful to day-to-day activity and interactions with others, it comes with a catch.

The more familiar we are with something, the harder it becomes for us to explain it and we tend to skip steps when sharing with others.

When a movement is repeated over time, a long-term muscle memory is created for that task, eventually allowing it to be performed without conscious effort. This process reduces the need for attention and maximizes efficiency within the motor and memory systems.

So, that's a good thing, right?

Yes, but...(you knew that was coming). When seeking the facts of a situation, the expert wired with muscle memory (think that super programmer, rock star salesperson, or buttoned-down scientist) may have a tendency to skip

Delivering Bad News in Good Ways:
Turn difficult conversations into purposeful dialogue, positive outcomes, & focused results in 3 easy steps

| 95 |

steps (information) because it is just so natural and ingrained for them that they assume everyone else knows it or that it is not that relevant or important.

▶ LEARNING = METHODS OF UNDERSTANDING

When teasing out the facts, it is important to use language and media with which the person is most comfortable. We will get into this more deeply when we consider the Deliver step of the SED Method in Chapter 7. For now, let's take a look at approach to questioning as it relates to teasing out the facts.

The idea that people are visual, auditory, or kinesthetic learners has been debated for a number of years. So many are convinced of its validity that a whole cottage industry evolved over the past few decades to support the different "learning styles."

In Patti Neighmond's 2011 article, *Think You're An Auditory Or Visual Learner? Scientists Say It's Unlikely,* Doug Rohrer, a psychologist at the University of South Florida, reviews studies on the subject and does not find sufficient evidence to qualify a difference. He said, *"Mixing things up is something we know is scientifically supported as something that boosts attention."*

While theory of learning styles is still out for review, using words that invoke a visual, auditory, or kinesthetic response is extremely helpful and one that marketers have used successfully for generations to help consumers connect with and promote product brands.

USING WORDS AS A PALETTE FOR CONTEXT

Let's start from the beginning. What was the first thing that happened?

When someone contacts you about a situation, they already have had time with it and are most likely several steps ahead of you, as illustrated with the example of my daughter's situation.

Asking **fact-based questions** gives you context for their situation and a chance to catch up while giving them a chance to step back from the subjective aspect of it.

For a better understanding of how this plays out on a project, let's take a look at how Sarah surprised Jim with using the Objective Question approach.

| 96 |

Delivering Bad News in Good Ways:
Turn difficult conversations into purposeful dialogue, positive outcomes, & focused results in 3 easy steps

When Sarah called about the latest status report, Jim anticipated she would have a lot of questions, and he knew he didn't have many answers. Sarah had a reputation for being really aggressive and directive on projects, so before discussing it with her, he "braced" himself for her characteristic machine gun approach.

Just as he took a deep breath to ready himself, she surprised him. Instead of bombarding him with conclusions, recriminations, and solutions to "get it fixed fast," Sarah kicked off the conversation with explaining why she called and then asked questions that showed genuine interest, curiosity, and a desire to understand the situation.

This new approach helped him relax and look at the issues noted in the status report in a different way. Sifting through the information born out of her questions, they were able to come up with a workable solution.

Asking Objective Questions has another benefit beyond providing the other person a chance to get their ideas and perspective out and giving you context for their experience. It gives you a chance to pause so you can figure out what to do in response while giving them a chance to slow down. The process gives you both an opportunity to get on the same page so you can partner on the next steps.

Delivering Bad News in Good Ways:
Turn difficult conversations into purposeful dialogue, positive outcomes, & focused results in 3 easy steps

| 97 |

BEFORE JUMPING IN, GET CLEAR WITH YOUR SELF

In Chapter 4 we took a high-level view of assessing the impact of bad news. Before jumping into a conversation about the bad news, it is important to understand *what it means to you* before determining what you should do next.

This will help you better manage your emotions so you can focus on doing what is right for the situation and not just on how you feel.

Consider the following questions originally posed in Chapter 4 about possible responses to hearing the bad news for the first time. I have added some responses for you to consider.

▶ What is your immediate emotional response - *Fear, dread, excitement, anger, sadness...*

▶ What impulse do you have? *Attack, withdraw, pull in other people, run away...*

▶ What change has your body experience in response? *Sweaty palms, stomach turns, heat in your chest...*

▶ Are you excited or scared? Path to opportunity, interruption of routine...

▶ Do you want to promote it or avoid it? *See possibilities or obstacles...*

▶ Do you want to host a pep rally-like meeting or does yelling and screaming at someone appeal to you? *Party or party-pooper*

▶ Do you just jump in and act or do you give yourself time before speaking? *Take the leap and worry later about the fall out! Pause, breathe, then speak...*

As noted earlier, our bodies **feel** our emotional response to the news before we are consciously **aware** of it. Since we are the sum total of our past, it is important to understand that your emotional response to a current situation evolved from experiences you had **long** before you entered your current job.

What does this mean relative to delivering bad news about your projects to stakeholders? If you do not get a handle on what the news means to you first, sharing the news with others will be all the more difficult. Let's start with moods.

| 98 |

Delivering Bad News in Good Ways:
Turn difficult conversations into purposeful dialogue, positive outcomes, & focused results in 3 easy steps

YOUR MIND ON MOODS

To get a handle on yourself, it is important to understand the mechanics of feelings. There are loads of other resources that do a solid job handling this subject in greater detail. If you are interested, I have listed some recommendations in at my website at *www.alisonsigmon.com/books/resources* that can help you do a deeper dive.

In the meantime, we will do a brief overview that should give you enough information to get clear with yourself before sharing bad news with others. This will help you recognize what you are experiencing so you can select the best course of action.

SUN, CLOUDS, OR SOMEWHERE IN BETWEEN – YOUR MIND AND MOODS

Quick…how do you feel **RIGHT NOW?** Do you feel a mood coming on? What's it like? Maybe it is that happy over-the-top feeling you hope lasts and lasts. Perhaps it is a prickly irritation or a slow boil that has you teetering on the edge of eruption. It could even be a state of calm that feels like a favorite food or plush pillow.

Whatever you are feeling, moods can make or break your day, but they are not always caused by just one thing. Moods are the result of a collection of things around you and inside you that become the houseguest you hope will stay forever or the interloper you fear will NEVER leave.

To get a grip on what you are experiencing, it is important to understand that emotions, moods, and traits are different. It is the stuff bubbling beneath the surface that spurs you into action, has you run in retreat, or leaves you standing still with shock.

What you are feeling also influences how you respond to events throughout your day. While they affect each other, emotions, moods, and traits are very different and play into your day-to-day experience.

Delivering Bad News in Good Ways:
Turn difficult conversations into purposeful dialogue, positive outcomes, & focused results in 3 easy steps

| 99 |

EMOTIONS ARE FLEETING

They may last for mere seconds or hang in for a few minutes, but either way they are an immediate response to something. Sights, smells, sounds, and events can set them off. Memories from the past or thoughts about future can trigger an emotion as well.

A few years ago I took my daughter to meet up with some of our extended family who had all gathered for a small reunion in New York City. We had a great time crawling around the city enjoying the many sights and sounds it offers, and while we had a large group, everything went off without issue until we got to the airport.

I thought my daughter was right behind me, but when I got through security, I saw she was not there. I walked around the corner to the beginning of the line and saw she was being held there. When I asked the representative what was going on, he informed me that her roller bag was too large to carry onto the plane.

We flew out with her bag as a carry on and had done so successfully on past trips, but this gentleman refused to let us carry it on this time because it did not fit the tester. Well, it was obvious that few of the other roller bags fit the tester – and one traveler even quoted the TSA rule for size – but to no avail.

Inside at that moment, my emotional state went from calm and happy because I was having such a nice time with my family to deep frustration bordering on anger.

I felt it in my body first. I started feeling hot even though my jacket was appropriate for the season and the room temperature had not changed. I felt my face flush with heat and color. I felt the urge to get into the guy's personal space – to make him feel as uncomfortable as I felt. Basically, I wanted to attack with words. I used completely logical reasoning for why the bag should go forward, but he ignored me.

Feeling angry at this point, I marched (yes, nearly literally) down to the ticket counter where I experienced the same response. I recognized I was very close to making a scene that would not end well.

| 100 |

Delivering Bad News in Good Ways:
Turn difficult conversations into purposeful dialogue, positive outcomes, & focused results in 3 easy steps

My ego wanted to win, but I did not have the authority or power to do so. I could feel a mood ready to set up house in my head, which would affect the rest of my day. So I backed off. It simply was not worth it, even though I knew the bag fit just like all the other bags they did allow through.

Feeling back in control I elected to check both our roller bags. Being a "glass half full" kind of person, I decided to see the upside of checking the bags – unencumbered, easy to move, no lifting, and ability to move faster if we needed to. When my daughter and I caught up with my family, we discussed it briefly.

My cousin said he would not let such a thing ruin his day. I agreed. Nor would I, but I had to concede that little things like that are very irritating to me and can set me off quickly because there is no logic to it and the other person will not listen.

The reality is the workers were following the rules to the letter and I did not like it. It was my problem, not theirs.

My cousin was right. A situation like this could ruin a person's day if they let it. One event can put us on notice to watch for other situations like it, which then would "confirm" an expectation that more experiences like the first one are "bound" to happen.

It is like collecting – at some point we go looking for things that validate the initial belief. You get enough of a collection of something then in our minds it gets knitted together into a pattern that informs an expectation or belief.

This is what happens with moods. Instead of forming an expectation in my head about how the remainder of the day would go based this event, I chose to see it as an isolated incident. This attitude freed me to see other events of the day as individual occurrences as opposed to events that validated the primary emotion I was feeling from the bag event.

Instead of saying, "It's just my luck," "It figures that happened," or "All airline and government employees are jerks (which they are not)," I chose to look at the broader picture – I had not had that experience at other airports, it was insignificant to the other activities that needed to happen that day to get home, and I do not have to be right all the time.

Delivering Bad News in Good Ways:
Turn difficult conversations into purposeful dialogue, positive outcomes, & focused results in 3 easy steps

| 101 |

What is important about this process is awareness and acknowledgement. Awareness puts us in touch with the moment so we can use the information as part of our assessment of the situation.

Acknowledgement allows us to recognize the feeling as valid but not become a slave to it where we have to act on it when not appropriate.

Basically, it is like counting to 10 like our moms did in response to an event. Counting lets us recognize the event but then gives our rational brain a chance to catch up so the emotion of the event does not hijack us into reacting and doing something we might regret. Said before but good to revisit (often)!

But what happens when we see events like this as a collection? The risk is it fuels a mood...

| 102 |

Delivering Bad News in Good Ways:
Turn difficult conversations into purposeful dialogue, positive outcomes, & focused results in 3 easy steps

MOODS LAST FOR HOURS OR DAYS

A mood is brought on by a series of events or activities, and can last for hours or days, typically. They tend to be directed at the world rather than toward a particular thing.

Moods change for a number of reasons — something building up with your boss, the type of weather, hormonal shifts, issue at home, not enough sleep or exercise, or too much caffeine or sugar. And if it seems some people are more prone to moodiness, you would be correct with that assumption.

People are different and in particular the **genders** are different. For example, the male brain on average produces **52 percent more serotonin**, a chemical that affects mood, than the female brain. This difference likely explains why men and women respond differently to dramas and love stories and why having a bad day can be harder for women to bounce back from time-to-time.

Another difference involves hormonal changes. Louann Brizendine, M.D. notes in her book, **The Female Brain,** that that some parts of a woman's brain can change up to **25 percent** during a given month due to hormone shifts. Other life issues can exacerbate these changes.

To avoid overreacting to a spontaneous barb from a colleague or loved one, take a step back and breathe. We may not be consciously aware of it, but we all bring the emotional baggage of a day into the room, so don't make your first assumption your conclusion when you look at a person's face or hear their tone of voice.

While there is an internal chemical component involved in the process of developing a mood, behavior or response is just as important to the process.

Take the bag situation I mentioned earlier. My frustration with the event could have kicked off the activity of me "looking" for other events in the day that would extend and deepen that initial frustration which then could have created a mood.

In other words, if my response was, "it figures...this always happens," then I would have likely looked (or created) other situations where that feeling and belief was validated.

Delivering Bad News in Good Ways:
Turn difficult conversations into purposeful dialogue, positive outcomes, & focused results in 3 easy steps

| 103

What this means is then I can be right even if I do not like the feeling or result. As odd as that may sound, it does give us some sense of being in control even when the result is undesirable.

This is the risk we must watch out for in the **Separate** step of **SED**. When we hear bad news or what is perceived as bad news, it is tempting to personalize it as if the event is specifically directed at you. This feeling is more exaggerated based on other events of the day or what is happening on a hormonal level.

It also plays out when we feel we do not have much control in our lives during the time the event takes place. This is a deeper subject more suitable for self-help and psychology, but it is important to understand that we can influence how we think and respond to something and the event does not have to result in a lingering mood.

| 104 |

Delivering Bad News in Good Ways:
Turn difficult conversations into purposeful dialogue, positive outcomes, & focused results in 3 easy steps

ATTITUDE HELPS TO SEPARATE

What helps with this is self-talk and optimism. Martin Seligman, considered by many to be the "father" of a branch of psychology called Positive Psychology, pioneered research and writing about optimism over the past few decades.

What he and other researchers found is that what we say to ourselves and others influences how we feel, think, and behave.

As a project manager, why should you care?

How you interpret what you hear and see and how you talk about it can influence how others respond to it.

Assume, for example, you have just heard some bad news about your project schedule. A major issue surfaced that will add two weeks to your project timeline. Of course, this is bad, but what is worse at this point is that the project is already three weeks in delay. Using the questions below, assess your initial response:

▶ Does it feel like the end of the world or just a speed bump?

▶ Do you see it as "more bad luck" or simply a moment in time?

▶ Does it feel like "things will never change" or a curious puzzle to figure out?

The response you chose for each may offer insight into your attitude about change, challenges, etc. Now, this is just a single event.

Thinking back on events that are similar to the one described above, did you have a similar response? If you did, then we might have a pattern in play. If you did not, then the difference simply could be your current state of mind.

▶ If there seems to be a pattern, then this could be a hint at your attitude about events in life, but what does that mean?

▶ If you selected "end of the world, "more bad luck," "things will never change," in response to the questions, then your attitude likely is more pessimistic.

Delivering Bad News in Good Ways:
Turn difficult conversations into purposeful dialogue, positive outcomes, & focused results in 3 easy steps

| 105 |

▶ If you selected just a "speed bump," "moment in time," or a "curious puzzle to figure out," in response to the questions, then your attitude is likely more optimistic.

Some people view a situation as permanent and unchangeable. Others view a situation as temporary and specific. The thoughts that pop into your head upon hearing or seeing an event offer some insight on your perspective.

When you have a more optimistic view, you tend to view situations as temporary and specific. When your view leans towards pessimism, you tend to view situations as more permanent and universal, and you may even personalize situations that do not pertain to you.

As mentioned previously, managing change is a big part of what you do as a project manager, and your attitude about change impacts how stakeholders see and respond to it. Change often follows what is perceived as "bad news," and your attitude about it can influence the outcome.

Checking your mood when you hear the "bad" news and paying attention to how you talk to yourself about it will help you get a handle on yourself first — before involving others.

Now, that was a simple exercise to understand your typical point of view, but there is a bit more to helping you separate so you can respond to bad news in the most appropriate way.

Assessing your attitude and beliefs does not have to take years of therapy. It can be as simple as being more aware of words used, routines, and habits through observing yourself and paying attention to comments from others.

| 106 |

Delivering Bad News in Good Ways:
Turn difficult conversations into purposeful dialogue, positive outcomes, & focused results in 3 easy steps

A LITTLE SELF-AWARENESS GOES A L-O-N-G WAY...

When I am teaching workshops that involve this subject, invariably there will be some subtle squirms in seats and quick looks away at nothing in particular.

In the corporate space, being emotional and showing our emotions tends make people feel uncomfortable, and this discomfort tends to result in raised eyebrows, exaggerated eye rolls, or sarcastic remarks.

What is ironic about this response is that it is the emotional connection we forge with project stakeholders that typically motivates everyone to band together to get work done.

Because project managers often find themselves managing projects without authority over the stakeholders, it is their savvy ability to read and understand the emotions of others that help the project manager build rapport and influence them to do what needs to be done on the project.

Before a project manager can successfully "read" the emotional pulse of a situation or a person, they first must have a deeper understanding of themselves.

In addition to optimistic and pessimistic attitudes, understanding is also comprised of having an awareness of what behaviors, actions, and events can trigger a response that might not be suitable. This awareness gives you a chance to create self-management methods that help you act and not react.

I remember a situation years ago where I was talking with a person about the state of his company. It had undergone a series of massive changes that restructured the entire business. Before the restructuring, the company had a series of missteps that left them bleeding cash and in need of rebuilding their client base. The process took a couple of years to be fully realized.

In the meantime, layoffs and reassignments left the employees feeling a bit shell shocked as they felt their way through the many new relationships that were created as a result of the reorganization.

Delivering Bad News in Good Ways:
Turn difficult conversations into purposeful dialogue, positive outcomes, & focused results in 3 easy steps

| 107 |

Although the employees were fully behind the changes, it deeply affected the culture and sense of security. The gentleman who approached me wanted to discuss the new boss he had as a result of the reorganization. He recounted several exchanges they had over a few months, and it was clear by his demeanor that he was not happy about the new relationship.

I asked him some questions in an effort to discern what he really wanted from the discussion and how I could help. His biggest complaint seemed to be about the difference in style between his former boss and his new boss. He said the new guy "really gets under my skin," "rubs me the wrong way," and "definitely pushes my buttons."

He admitted this had resulted in him doing and saying some things that he was not "feeling good or proud" about having done. Homing in on the word "buttons," I asked him what "definitely pushes my buttons" meant and looked like to him.

It took a couple of minutes but then with a very red face he replied, "I don't having any idea, but he SURE does PUSH them!"

I continued to work with him to get clear on what was behind his response to the new boss's style. When we started our discussion it was clear his awareness of himself needed some work because without knowing his "buttons," he left himself vulnerable to a kind of "emotional hijacking" that left him feeling bad about his response to his boss.

Emotional hijacking was mentioned briefly earlier in this chapter. It is when a person responds to situations without thinking about them, which often leads to making bad choices and ineffective responses, losing credibility with team members, and feeling chronic dissatisfaction with their situation and their work.

Getting right with yourself first is to Separate in the SED Method.

| 108 |

Delivering Bad News in Good Ways:
Turn difficult conversations into purposeful dialogue, positive outcomes, & focused results in 3 easy steps

KNOW YOUR BUTTONS

Self-awareness like this takes time and focus, and a deep dive into this subject is outside the scope of this book; however, a brief overview of methods that can help you focus and understand situations and actions that "push your buttons" will help you manage your response and deliver bad news on your project.

Let's take a look at Jamal and his situation to assess how to grow awareness of your "buttons" so they are less likely to get pushed.

Buried in a sea of spreadsheets for what seemed like hours, Jamal knew he was only putting off the inevitable. Countless meetings with the development team and the tech vendor along with doing the math for the schedule and the budget made it obvious.

Quite simply, the project, which had been going for what felt like a very long six months, needed to be shut down. Now.

His stomach turned a few back flips as he shifted uncomfortably in his seat.

Any way they sliced the numbers it just could not be salvaged. The mountain of discussions about the work completed and not completed to date and the mounting delivery issues underscored the need to stop throwing money and people at this.

Heat welled up in his chest and neck. He ran his index finger around the inside of his collar in an attempt to loosen it, but it was already loose.

Throughout the project, the sponsor pushed the team even when Jamal felt in his gut it was not realistic. His project experience over the years had taught him how to quickly separate the dogs from the stars.

The product they were developing with this project was a dog right out of the gate because of the inexperience with the technology and whispers that a new version of this technology would be released next year, which would render this project obsolete.

Sweat now peppered his forehead. He wiped his brow with the back of his hand.

Delivering Bad News in Good Ways:
Turn difficult conversations into purposeful dialogue, positive outcomes, & focused results in 3 easy steps

| 109 |

Several times he had shared with the sponsor his feelings about the project and the deep research he done to back up his position, but the sponsor just kept saying he felt the team could get on the other side of the current issues if they tried harder.

Jamal repeatedly presented a ton of validated testing to the contrary. So convinced this product would catapult the company to the next level in their industry, the sponsor told him to "press on" with it.

A dull headache settled on him. He reached for some aspirin.

Jamal wanted to figuratively choke the unreasonable sponsor. His frustration with the situation was close to a breaking point for him.

Impulsively he swept up all the documents into his arms and proceeded straight down to the sponsor's office, not caring if he was busy or not.

Jamal knew when this project failed he and the team would be the scapegoats. He'd seen this happen before with this sponsor. He was less concerned about himself and more concerned about the demoralization and possible smear on the people on the team as a result of the failure.

Leaning into his walk and picking up his pace, he found himself just about to step into the sponsor's office, intending to give him a piece of his mind.

As he reached for the doorknob, he saw his hand was shaking. He held his breath for a few seconds and backed away from the door.

In that moment he saw he was in no shape to meet with the sponsor now. Suddenly a memory from a similar experience on a project from years ago flashed across his mind.

He had made a big mistake back then, and now he saw all the signs that he was about to make the same mistake again. He knew he needed to take a step back and cool off in order to wrap his head around how best to deal with this in a way that the sponsor could really hear.

HOW JAMAL KNEW...

| 110 |

Delivering Bad News in Good Ways:
Turn difficult conversations into purposeful dialogue, positive outcomes, & focused results in 3 easy steps

Fortunately for Jamal and his team, he was able to recognize the signs of an impending emotional hijacking.

In Chapter 4 we established that the hippocampus, which is reportedly the seat of memory, and the amygdala, the memory processor and emotions regulator, tag team to form your emotional response to anything you experience. Typically it is our bodies that give us a first clue about how we feel in response to something.

Because of our individual experiences, people respond differently. Whereas someone else in Jamal's shoes might have had a casual attitude about the situation, it clearly affected him on a very deep level because his body was so involved. This variation of response stems from early experiences, as we reviewed in the Thinking Process at the beginning of this chapter.

We learn to interpret our world and communicate with others long before we learn to speak. As babies we drank in the world around us and cleverly figured out what we needed to do to get our needs met. Events we experienced along the way shaped who we are today.

Because it is so simple, it is attractive to think that at some point in our early development the person we become is fixed, but science has demonstrated that is not the case. As it turns out, our personalities are more fluid than we think.

A study spearheaded by Jordi Quoidbach, Daniel T. Gilbert, and Timothy D. Wilson and published in the *Journal Science,* looked at a phenomenon called "end of history illusion," which is how we tend to underestimate amount we will change over a lifetime.

The findings of the study, which involved 19,000 people ages 18 to 68, turned on its ear the idea that we have fixed personalities.

What is more curious (and revealing) is that we can see how much we have changed in the past and yet we typically do not see the potential for how we will change in the future. In other words, we can see in hindsight how we have changed, but tend to not believe we will change much in the future.

Events and experiences occur over a lifetime, so it is safe to assume that

Delivering Bad News in Good Ways:
Turn difficult conversations into purposeful dialogue, positive outcomes, & focused results in 3 easy steps

| 111 |

they will affect how we view and interact with the world. In Jamal's case, the recalled past project experience helped him recognize he was traveling down a path that did not work when a similar event happened the first time.

In both experiences, Jamal was an adult, which means he was not the same "impulsive" person that he was years before in situations like this because he was able to recognize and interrupt his initial response to the situation.

The upside of this is that we are not and do not have to be bound to our preverbal experiences or subsequent past experiences.

It is clear that Jamal had developed the ability to **assess** his current situation, **reflect** and think about the event, and gain **insight** that helped him form new behaviors and responses based on the new and improved information.

In this chapter we have considered how to assess the situation and separate fact from opinion with others and within ourselves.

Reflection and insight are important to personal growth but also critical when addressing business problems.

In the next chapter we will consider reflective and interpretative questions as part of the Evaluate step of the SED model.

CHAPTER TAKEAWAYS

▶ Objective questioning

▶ Don't make your first assumption your conclusion

▶ Watch your mental models -- Don't jump to label it

▶ Do a head check and gut check before pulling others in

▶ You get back what you put out there

▶ Know your buttons

| 112 |

Delivering Bad News in Good Ways:
Turn difficult conversations into purposeful dialogue, positive outcomes, & focused results in 3 easy steps

CHAPTER 6:

EVALUATE STEP OF THE SED METHOD

CONNECTING THE DOTS

LIGHTS, CAMERA, ACTION! LOOK BEFORE YOU LEAP

This was not the first time Irina had faced this kind of situation. As a serial startup employee, she was well familiar with the financial roller coaster experience typical of early ventures.

The entertainment and commerce production company wasn't doing something that had not been done before, but they were doing it in a vertical where it had not been done successfully. The team was determined to be the first.

Her first six months with the startup moved at a fast pace. Processes were put into place, new people were on boarded, digital platforms were upgraded, and new broadcast slots were added to the schedule.

Things seemed to be going well, but Irina soon learned that was not the case. The startup was running dangerously low on cash. As it turns out, this was the first of two critical cash flow moments during her time with the startup.

The first time it happened, the CEO contacted her about the cash crunch almost immediately. In an effort to grasp the current state, she asked several questions similar to what we reviewed in the SEPARATE step of the SED model. Once she had the facts and projections, she put the following on the table:

▸ Probability of securing the anticipated funds

▸ Amount needed and time estimated to secure the funds

▸ What cash support was needed for that time gap

▸ Who should be made aware of the situation

The CEO assured Irina that it would only be two pay periods for a total of one month before the money would be deposited from the new investor. He also projected that cash flow from existing sources would be enough to pay most of the staff.

He suggested the leadership team take half pay or no pay for the one-month timeframe to give the company an operating buffer. His dilemma and the

| 114 |

Delivering Bad News in Good Ways:
Turn difficult conversations into purposeful dialogue, positive outcomes, & focused results in 3 easy steps

reason he contacted Irina was whether or not to tell the entire staff about the situation.

Based on what he said, it appeared he had sufficiently modeled out the risk and response options and that the situation would be temporary. If it was temporary then involving the entire staff could impact morale and be a distraction from the work they needed to do to be solvent and stable.

Based on her evaluation of the CEO's financial projections, the upward trending response in current revenue streams, and alternatives identified should funding fall through, it seemed a sensible plan.

Funding was secured as estimated and the leadership team was caught up on its suspended payments. The evaluation and consequent decision to withhold the bad news from the staff turned out to be the right thing to do. People were able to stay focused and continue to build critical mass for the business.

As we will learn later in this chapter, Irina and the CEO had to circle back to this situation when the same issue cropped up again later in the year. But more about that after we look at how she moved from the fact-gathering Separate step of the SED Method to the Evaluate step.

First we will look at a process for sorting through our own feelings and thoughts and those of people who are potentially affected by the bad news. Then we will consider how to organize and prioritize that information in preparation for the Deliver step of the SED Method.

Delivering Bad News in Good Ways:
Turn difficult conversations into purposeful dialogue, positive outcomes, & focused results in 3 easy steps

| 115 |

SEPARATE TO EVALUATE

Separating gives us a chance to investigate and collect the facts, opinions, and details of the situation so we can act rather than react to challenging situations.

The Evaluate step gives us time to sort through that information, determine what is relevant, and identify options in preparation for delivery of the bad news to the receiver.

Evaluation is an important but often glossed over step in delivering bad news. This step moves us through emotional acknowledgement (feeling brain) to rational, logical processing (thinking brain). It involves the following:

▶ **Assessing** your thoughts and feelings – emotion, attitude, triggers

▶ **Anticipating** team thoughts and feelings – emotion, impact, response

▶ **Impact** on the work – time, cost, scope

▶ **Options** based on scenario modeling

In the first installment of Irina's story, she and the CEO worked through evaluating and determining how best to managing the cash flow issue. In that situation, they identified the facts and evaluated the best course of action given the circumstances.

What the narrative does not reveal to the reader is what was happening for them on an emotional level. Clearly they were able to manage their feelings about the situation and come up with a thoughtful course of action.

How did they do that?

How were they able to work past their own emotional experience?

They were not robots, as we will see. Let's take a look at what likely was going on behind the scenes.

| 116 |

Delivering Bad News in Good Ways:
Turn difficult conversations into purposeful dialogue, positive outcomes, & focused results in 3 easy steps

ASSESSING THOUGHTS AND FEELINGS: START WITH YOU

If it is not a life or death situation, jumping in and acting on your first assumption could be the equivalent of driving off a cliff. The wiser course of action is to slow down and stop short of the cliff, but that requires awareness of yourself and your inclinations.

Awareness requires pause and presence.

While it is impractical to be aware of every single thought and feeling we have every minute of every day (nor do we want to!), it is very practical to pause when an event creates a change in our physical and emotional state.

Using the objective questions we reviewed in the previous chapter, we create a pause to collect the facts of the event that spawned the change we have just experienced.

Asking questions gives your mind and body time to slow down.

We have already established that our body and emotions respond faster than our mind, so taking stock of the information can give us time to decide what to do in response (if anything at all). Let's take an example.

You are sitting at your desk at your desk and your phone rings. Caller ID tells you it is the sponsor for one of your ailing projects.

Put yourself in that moment. Now…

▶ What do you notice about your body?

▶ Are you suddenly flushed with heat?

▶ Do you feel a pick-up in your pulse?

▶ Do you shift in your seat?

Do not bother with thinking about what the things you notice about your body mean. Just make note of it.

When you answer the phone, the normally chipper project sponsor has a very direct tone. In a flat, monotone voice that is so different from his

Delivering Bad News in Good Ways:
Turn difficult conversations into purposeful dialogue, positive outcomes, & focused results in 3 easy steps

| 117 |

typical animated, engaging style, he tells you he has seen the report you sent last night that shows the most recent expenses.

Here are the facts leading up to this phone call.

Because of a recent change, more money was spent for the additional work required from the vendor. Without the expenditure, the project timeline would be extended by two months, which the sponsor deemed unacceptable.

You informed the sponsor verbally and via email of the additional expense prior to the work starting. He told you to carry on with it. Back to the call…

You notice his tone is nagging at you. It is so different from how he usually is. You note your pulse rate is picking up and you feel a slight queasiness in your stomach.

Emotions offer a ton of information about others and ourselves. As examples, they alert us to what needs attention, stakeholders who have concerns, confusion among the team, or people who may lack commitment to the objectives.

Emotional self-awareness is another source of information about what is happening inside and around you, yet people tend to discount emotions at work as being of little value.

You did not stop being human just because you crossed the threshold of work. Neither did you stakeholders.

Taking stock of your emotional and physical response to what is happening around you gives you information that you may or may not act on. It is just a data point considered on a continuum of information.

Let's consider this through the lens of the phone call example.

At this point in the exchange it is tempting to jump to a conclusion about the sponsor's behavior instead of looking at the facts.

Labeling his tone as *"flat, monotone,"* and noticing how it is "*so different from his typical animated, engaging style,*" could lead you down the path of

| 118 |

Delivering Bad News in Good Ways:
Turn difficult conversations into purposeful dialogue, positive outcomes, & focused results in 3 easy steps

personalizing the situation when you simply do not have enough information to make that determination.

You may be right in your assumption, but at this point it is just an opinion and therefore only good as a piece of information in a collection.

This is an important activity in the **Evaluate** step of the SED Method. It is the ability to watch yourself without labeling it. This means you figuratively step outside yourself and watch what you pay attention to in the moment.

You consider the thoughts, feelings, and questions that pop into your mind over the course of your day or related to a specific event. You observe how you interact with others.

It is through these moments that you gain deeper understanding of who you are at your core – your values, beliefs, boundaries, passions, character, moods, tendencies, verbal and behavioral inconsistencies, aspirations, and patterns.

Okay, before it begins to feel like we're headed for the therapist's couch, let's back up.

Observing yourself gives you a chance to identify your triggers (pushed buttons) — what can "set you off" in a heartbeat. Being aware of your triggers will help you recognize them as they pop up so you can manage them and talk yourself back from the cliff of reaction.

And who is the manager of these triggers/buttons? I think you already know…

There is a little voice inside of us that feeds the inner dialogue. Psychologists call it "self-talk." It is self-talk that gives your cortical (thinking) brain a chance to jump in before your limbic (feeling) brain acts like a bull in a china shop.

It is where you coach, question, and mentor yourself. It is also an opportunity to challenge your assumptions.

As we previously established, we all are great fiction writers. In the absence of information, we usually make it up.

Delivering Bad News in Good Ways:
Turn difficult conversations into purposeful dialogue, positive outcomes, & focused results in 3 easy steps

| 119 |

Observing ego (that's psych speak for watching your own behavior) and using self-talk gives us a chance to gut-check the stories we tell ourselves. Not having this internal meter can wreak havoc on our emotional self and emotional relationships with others.

Okay, so we can watch ourselves and take note of how we are feeling, but then what?

Will that keep us from driving off the ledge?

Um, no…that is just the first part of a process.

To know our "buttons" in difficult situations, we have to evaluate and learn from those observations. This requires reflection, which leads to insight, as we will see next.

| 120 |

Delivering Bad News in Good Ways:
Turn difficult conversations into purposeful dialogue, positive outcomes, & focused results in 3 easy steps

HINDSIGHT IS 20/20
REFLECTION – LOOKING BACK TO LIVE FORWARD

"Life can only be understood backwards; but it must be lived forwards."
~ Søren Kierkegaard

Consider these scenarios...

Imagine you have just kicked back in your chair with something to drink. Your mind wanders to a conversation you had with a colleague earlier in the week about a situation on your project.

When on a long walk, you go over in your head the performance feedback you gave recently to a team member.

You are scanning your daily news feeds and your eye lands on an article that is about taking risks. You begin to think about a shaky risk you took years ago.

COLLECT AND CONNECT THE DOTS

If you have not experienced these exact situations noted above, it is still easy to relate. When you cruise a memory, you are looking back as if you are looking into a mirror. In that mirror you can examine, look at the details, and maybe see things you had not noticed previously.

Quite simply, reflection is a pause, which is important in the hectic day-to-day activity of life. It is inside that pause that your mind can relax and review an event much like watching a film clip or segment of a TV show.

This is somewhat like a form of meditation where you objectively watch what passes through your mind. The key to the success of reflection is being objective – to let the event replay in your head without labeling it or responding to it emotionally.

Reflection is deeply important to the learning process.

Delivering Bad News in Good Ways:
Turn difficult conversations into purposeful dialogue, positive outcomes, & focused results in 3 easy steps

| 121 |

This reminds me of when I was in graduate school. It always seemed there was so much to learn and too little time to learn it. I constantly crammed as much information from as many sources as I possibly could, but it was not long before I realized that this method did not help me deeply retain and integrate it.

Basically, I was doing rote learning, which simply means I memorized information but did not always think critically about how and when to use it. I was not considering how the new information enhanced what I already knew. So I changed my tactic...

I started going for a run after study sessions.

It was during these runs that I would "look" at what I had learned. I would ask questions to myself about it. I would wonder how a certain concept fit (or did not fit) with what I already knew.

Ah-ha...using the filter process noted in Chapter 5!

It was during these reflective times that I began to really understand what I was learning and to integrate it as part of a deep well that I could draw on as I faced situations, problems, and opportunities.

Reflection is very important to critical thinking. It is critical thinking that helps us come up with new ideas, to innovate, and to solve problems.

Critical thinking helps us to deepen self-awareness and identify patterns that help us to get out of our own way. In her book, **Teaching to the brain's natural learning systems,** Barbara K. Givens has this to say this about reflective thinking:

"Reflective thinking involves personal consideration of one's own learning. It considers personal achievements and failures and asks what worked, what didn't, and what needs improvement. It asks the learner to think about her own thinking."

Reflection takes place after an event, and it gives us time to process what we have seen or heard. It is an opportunity to look at a situation through a more present, less emotional lens.

We review what was said, how we felt, and what the other person or people involved did. We break down the sequence of events and assess the twists and turns of the experience. Reflection also gives us an opportunity to make sure we did not miss anything when we heard or saw it the first time.

Delivering Bad News in Good Ways:
Turn difficult conversations into purposeful dialogue, positive outcomes, & focused results in 3 easy steps

| 123 |

OUR MONKEY MIND & STORYTELLING

Buddhists have a concept called "Monkey Mind," in which our minds have a tendency to bounce from thought to thought, which can create discomfort and even sometimes anxiousness.

It is through reflection that we can slow the mind and observe our thought process.

Observation gives us a chance to see what we tend to focus on, how that focus influences our emotional state, and the thoughts and ideas that get spawned as a result.

It also relaxes our mind so we can see what we did not catch the first time round. This opportunity to re-evaluate allows us to step back from the situation so we learn from it and get some understanding for next steps.

Another big benefit of reflection is it can help us manage the stories we tell ourselves about past situations. It is natural to make assumptions in the absence of information as we have already established. It is such an important activity in project management that the Project Management Institute (PMI) fully integrated the activity into its publication the *Project Management Body of Knowledge.*

According to PMI, assumptions are considered to be true or certain until otherwise proven. When managing projects we are expected to make assumptions throughout the lifecycle because there is a great deal we do not know as we facilitate the development of a product or service.

The activity comes with a responsibility to check our assumptions. We are expected to check and recheck our assumptions and to purge assumptions that are proven to not be true.

The pitfall of making assumptions is we can get attached to them (remember emotional investment?).

When your project's sponsor seems distracted and has poor eye contact while you are giving a status update, you may assume he is unhappy with your project when in reality he had a difficult call with a business partner or a family member, and he is still thinking about it.

| 124 |

Delivering Bad News in Good Ways:
Turn difficult conversations into purposeful dialogue, positive outcomes, & focused results in 3 easy steps

If you hang on to that assumption, it may drive you to say or do something that is not necessary or could even be harmful to your project and your relationship.

Once the meeting is over, if you think back (reflect) on it, you might recall that your sponsor was just hanging up the phone and had a very puzzled, perplexed look on his face. You might also remember it took a few seconds for it to register that you were standing in the doorway.

Reflection with objectivity can reveal new information in the form of insights. The trick is managing your Monkey Mind and the stories you create to explain what you think you see or hear. As we reviewed in a previous chapter, we bring our mental models to the table when we make assumptions.

While we have to make assumptions in the absence of information, we have to be careful not to be attached to them. In other words, when new information invalidates an assumption, we must let it go of it to move forward. You will actually feel better it you do. It is hard work and burns a lot of energy to maintain an invalidated belief.

Reflection is used to problem-solve, test, and evaluate. Focus on the facts of the event and discussion to discover things you might have missed when it happened. At this point you are the investigator watching the sequence of events at the scene.

Once you have reviewed it, you can decide what action, if any, the situation needs. It is through reflection that we can gain clarity and insight about the situation, our behavior, what action we need to take as a result, and what we can do differently should something similar happen again in the future.

Remember the Thinking Process explained in Chapter 5? You may have noticed that reflection is a step in moving through that process.

Delivering Bad News in Good Ways:
Turn difficult conversations into purposeful dialogue, positive outcomes, & focused results in 3 easy steps

| 125 |

REFLECTING ON THOUGHTS AND FEELINGS

The reflection-to-insight process as described above is not that different from what happens when considering the thoughts and feelings of others.

Reflection is facilitated through questioning yourself, but when slightly tweaked, you can use it when talking to others about the situation.

In the Separate step we looked at the ORID model for generating discussion by using objective questions to establish context and facts. Now, as part of the Evaluate step, we want to pull in feelings to expand understanding.

It typically starts with questions that consider the past, inside, outside, and future states. To help with this process, consider the **Reflective Questions** below for each instance.

▶ PAST STATE

- What past experience have I had that is similar to this experience?

- What did I do to address that experience?

- Was what I did it successful?

- If it was unsuccessful in the past what can I do differently this time?

▶ INSIDE STATE

- How do I feel about this situation?

- What are my concerns?

- Does this excite or scare me?

- What is my goal for this situation?

▶ OUTSIDE STATE

- What do I know about this situation?

- What are the possible blind spots? What can I infer?

- What are the opportunities?

- What are the risks?

- Are there others who can (or need) to help me with this?

| 126 |

Delivering Bad News in Good Ways:
Turn difficult conversations into purposeful dialogue, positive outcomes, & focused results in 3 easy steps

▶ What are the options given the circumstances?

▶ What could get in the way of addressing/solving this situation?

▶ Based on your experience with the team members how might each of them feel?

▶ FUTURE

▶ What is the best I can hope for?

▶ What is the least I can live with?

▶ What do I want to get them to agree to?

▶ If it could be done over, what would I change?

▶ Based on this situation, what are one to two things I would like to improve going forward?

You might be thinking, "That's a lot of questions!" and wondering where we are going with all these questions.

I agree - I am beginning to wonder myself...just kidding.

Yes, there are a lot of questions, and you may not need to use all of them. They are available to facilitate your thinking through the reflection process. If a question is not relevant, then skip it for the next.

You do not have to spend a ton of time with these questions, and you might want to roll through them with someone/a few people. The important thing is to do it.

This is how we organize what we know so we can sniff out patterns and needs. The Eureka! moment may hit you with a bang or a whimper. Oh, and what you thought was an Eureka! could be a false start, as we will see next.

Whatever the case, you have the information you need to glean insights that will inform the last step of the SED Method: **Deliver.**

For now, let's explore the process of insight. We will consider what can get in the way and how you can overcome it so you (hopefully) will not follow the wrong path or get stuck in a false start.

Delivering Bad News in Good Ways:
Turn difficult conversations into purposeful dialogue, positive outcomes, & focused results in 3 easy steps

| 127 |

EUREKA! FROM REFLECTION TO INSIGHT

"There is nothing so terrible as activity without insight."
~Johann Wolfgang von Goethe

WHY CONNECTING THE DOTS IS IMPORTANT TO THE SED MODEL PROCESS

Insight is that moment of clarity when something is understood that was previously confusing or confounding. It can occur in an instant like a flash or it can be a slow boil where the parts merge into something that makes sense as a whole. It can also be achieved alone or with a team.

Whatever form or method it takes, insight plays a valuable role in learning, communicating, and taking action. It is a deeper understanding of a situation that gives us ideas about how to proceed.

Insight naturally follows reflection. Where reflection gives us the opportunity to **observe and collect the dots,** insight gives us the understanding we need to **connect the dots** needed to respond.

It is through insight that we can determine what worked, what didn't work, and what could work so that we can determine next steps. It also enables us to integrate new ideas and information into our process in the event we end up in a similar situation in the future.

Consider these scenarios...

The conversation you had a few days ago with your project's main subject matter expert keeps playing in your mind. You tried what felt like a thousand different ways to explain why a feature he was adamant about could not be done. In the middle of the night you wake up understanding why you two could not align.

You're washing dishes while gazing out the window. You see a spider diligently working her web. Suddenly you see what you and the team have been missing with the new strategy you've employed for launching a product upgrade.

Watching the conversation like a film in your head, you begin to see where you got off track with selling your sponsor on a vital change to an operational process.

Insight involves the coalescence of multiple experiences and sources. As humans, we have the unique ability to do what psychologists call associative thinking.

Associative thinking helps us to connect the dots by tapping into a host of resources inside and around us. We might hit a museum, watch a kid work a puzzle, doodle, or listen to music much like Samir did in an earlier story.

The point is to think broadly, horizontally then cherry-pick the right experiences to go deep with solutions.

What influences your associative thinking lens? Lots of things!

Mood: If you are in a better mood you tend to have more success.

Basics: Lack of sleep, food, or your comfy blanket. Discomfort draws energy away from higher ordered interests and pursuits. So, get some sleep, eat healthy, and by all means take time to snuggle.

Breaks: Taking a break from the situation allows us the time needed to get on the other side of the shock, surprise, or frustration of what we have heard, experienced, or need to work through.

Location: Visiting a new place opens our mind to new possibilities which may help you see the situation in a new way.

Defense mechanisms: Review that list in Chapter 3. Something deeper might be in play — avoidance, procrastination, uncertainty.

Past experiences: Revisit those filters we reviewed in the Thinking Process outlined in Chapter 5.

Skills/Knowledge: Sometimes we simply do not know enough about the subject or situation so we need to dig in deeper.

Delivering Bad News in Good Ways:
Turn difficult conversations into purposeful dialogue, positive outcomes, & focused results in 3 easy steps

| 129 |

CLARIFY THE PROBLEM/OPPORTUNITY

You have got your facts lined up, dots collected and connected, and now, you might think you are ready to put that bad news out there.

But…hold off just a bit longer.

When under stress and pressure to "just do something," it is tempting to zip through this step of SED, but hold your horses. There is plenty of research that confirms not being deliberate in this step will likely not turn out well.

Take a moment to absorb this (again and again)…

Don't make your first assumption your conclusion

ROUNDING OUT EVALUATION

So far we have looked at the following:

▶ Clarified and interpreted the information you have collected

▶ Considered the assumptions you have made about the response of people affected by the bad news

The last part of the Evaluate step of SED is to identify options. It is this final part that will lead us to the Deliver step of the SED.

Distillation of options actually begins in the Separate step of the SED. Getting clear with our feelings and assessing the possible emotional response of affected team members allows us to get down to business with knowns, unknowns, and options.

Pulling in the output from the Separate step lays the groundwork for Evaluation. It is the Evaluate step that helps us get organized so we can assess options and create a go forward plan. Without it we risk not addressing the right problem at the right time.

Let's continue Irina's story to better understand the Evaluate step.

| 130 |

Delivering Bad News in Good Ways:
Turn difficult conversations into purposeful dialogue, positive outcomes, & focused results in 3 easy steps

LIGHTS, CAMERA, ACTION! LOOK BEFORE YOU LEAP: ROUND 2

The second financial crunch at the entertainment and ecommerce company was a completely different story.

Another round of funding was expected but was lagging. In the meantime, bills were piling up. The business had a strong holiday season for an ecommerce newbie in a very crowded field, but by January the climate shifted for the company.

The CEO seemed to be waffling on the money front in response to repeated questions from multiple team members, including Irina. After days and weeks of putting off a direct conversation about the state of the business, he finally took Irina's call. He disclosed concerns that cash flow wouldn't be enough to cover payroll. He asked her to look at what could be cut in ongoing expenses.

By February, the CFO told her the company was still struggling. She asked about the expected new round of funding. He said he was optimistic, but this time he was less confident about the timeframe in which it would be received.

Together they evaluated the options:

▶ Expected funding amount

▶ Projected income based on revenue streams

▶ Impact on the work and people

▶ Current attitude of employees and contractors

The more immediate expected amount was significantly less than the first cash crunch. Also, a pattern emerged around sales for production spots — the number sold per cycle and the fee charged were both too low to cover ongoing costs.

Production, which included mostly outsourced team time, equipment, and studio, was being done at cost which was supposed to be a temporary arrangement. The idea was to gradually pay more for production services without raising the fee for production spots as the business gained traction

Delivering Bad News in Good Ways:
Turn difficult conversations into purposeful dialogue, positive outcomes, & focused results in 3 easy steps

| 131 |

in the ecommerce space.

As time passed and analytics data was collected, it became clear that quick growth in ecommerce wouldn't happen as expected. It was simply was underfunded and competition was too stiff. This meant the current model was not sustainable. It also meant promises made to production staff couldn't be met.

Irina knew the CFO's income estimate was extremely optimistic considering the company's place in its growth cycle. Although she wasn't involved in television time procurement, she knew it wasn't cheap.

She also knew the margins for product sales were lower than projected in the business plan, and those margins were constantly chipped away by discounts and sales in an effort to woo business in an already crowded digital retail space.

The evaluation of the current state, cash flow projections, and less predictable investment situation called for a different approach with the employees and contractors this time round.

The original five people who agreed to half pay or no pay stepped up to do it again just to get the company through the cash crunch. Each division head assessed where further cuts could be made, but at that point, much had already been cut to the bone so doing that proved difficult.

It was clear this round would take longer. The team had to be told. They had a right to know the critical state and should have the opportunity to decide if they wanted to continue with the group or move on to something else.

The company lost some people, which was perfectly understandable, but surprisingly and gratefully, they gained some really talented, experienced people willing to take the risk in trade for lowered fees and stock.

Before informing the team, the leaders evaluated the impact of the news. The leadership team was clear the message had to be positioned honestly and simply. They also knew they needed to reinforce with empathy the understanding that people needed to make the best decision for them whether or not to continue working in the current unpredictable environment.

| 132 |

Delivering Bad News in Good Ways:
Turn difficult conversations into purposeful dialogue, positive outcomes, & focused results in 3 easy steps

They identified contingencies based on who might stay or go. Modeling scenarios based on cash flow and resources enabled them to thoughtfully prepare to share the company's current state with the team.

The process they used to evaluate the bad news situation was critical to delivery and to how the team responded. Irina and the other members of the leadership team spent a few days reviewing cash flow numbers to ensure they had considered all the options -- projecting the sales pipeline, going over the accounts payable and receivable, and requirements for daily operations.

It was critical to identify superfluous expenses in an effort to keep as many people at full pay as possible. Morale and retention were top of mind throughout the evaluation process.

Irina and the leadership team realized the news might come as a complete shock because the ever-increasing workload and pace hid the real state of the business. Also, some people were completely unaware of the financial stress of the company.

ASKING INTERPRETIVE QUESTIONS

Delivery of the news required the leadership team to carefully plan. If they had not taken the time to evaluate the situation as they did, they had no doubt it would have had a very different outcome.

The following are considerations they evaluated before meeting with the team.

▶ Data -- location, budget, amenities

▶ Probabilities -- length of stay, income ratio

▶ People -- impact, interest, attitude (buy-in)

▶ Estimate -- timeframe, cost

▶ Contingencies -- best case, worst case, scenario modeling, risks

Evaluation requires careful, critical thinking. Often we mistake being flooded with images, emotions, and task ideas for critical thinking. Well, it is form of thinking, but it is a little more complicated than that.

Delivering Bad News in Good Ways:
Turn difficult conversations into purposeful dialogue, positive outcomes, & focused results in 3 easy steps

| 133 |

Let's test it out with a famous example.

Quick – answer this question:

A bat and ball together cost $1.10. The bat costs a dollar more than the ball. How much does the ball cost?

Did you instantly think "ten cents?" Well, that is not actually correct even though it may feel right, as Philip E. Tetlock and Dan Garner point out in their book **Superforecasting: The Art and Science of Prediction.**

Tetlock and Garner explain that this well-known problem is derived from the *Cognitive Reflection Test*. The word "reflection" is the key here. People have a tendency to move quickly in the decision-making process.

They assume they know the answer or solution without slowing down and thinking about it carefully – collecting evidence (Separate step in the SED!) and looking for patterns in the information.

If you see yourself reflected in that statement, don't worry – most people do it…even very brainy people! To make snap decisions is normal and natural. Research tells us that making quick decisions is a critical skill that advanced the survival of humans, but that preference does not always serve us well in modern times.

When in the Evaluate step of the SED, we are wise to slow down and reflect. Reflect, you say? Good thing we already talked about that earlier in this chapter!

It is tempting to seek out evidence in support our immediate hunch about the situation and then build stories around it to reinforce that hunch. This process is something that Daniel Kahneman and Amos Tversky wrote about in their book, **Thinking Slow and Fast.**

The framework, which they call System 1 and System 2, is an easy way to understand how conscious thought works.

System 1 never sleeps. Its on-demand presence is reassuring, particularly in a crisis situation. It is quick to provide answers that reinforce feeling in control of a situation.

| 134 |

Delivering Bad News in Good Ways:
Turn difficult conversations into purposeful dialogue, positive outcomes, & focused results in 3 easy steps

This is likely the source of our "intuitive" self.

System 2 steps in to consider the answer provided by System 1. What is tricky is that System 2 does not always show up. Or if it does, it is dismissed. It really depends how committed we are to our first impression.

What drives this? It comes back to our experiences and beliefs, which is likely no surprise at this point in the book.

Here are a few considerations you might experience when deciding whether or not to roll with your System 1 response or to pause (and listen) to System 2. See you can determine which of the following represents System 1 and System 2.

▶ In past situations like this I have always been right

▶ The other person seems more confident and knowledgeable so they must be right

▶ All I have learned tells me this is the correct answer

▶ I am supposed to know what to do, so I have to say something

▶ I don't have enough information to make a decision

Let's take a look at how the stories we create to reinforce our impression or hunch play out.

PIG OR A BEAR

Peter Blaber, author of **The Mission, The Men, and Me: Lessons From a Former Delta Force Commander,** had a problem. Deep in the woods of the Appalachian Mountains on the east coast of the United States for a military training mission, he felt under threat — from black bears.

Carrying a 75-pound rucksack while moving through thick vines and foliage, he heard sounds that he thought sounded like they came from a cub. In the dim light he saw dark movement in the distance.

Satisfied his eyes confirmed what his ears heard, he scrambled up a tree and waited it out for a LONG time. When he thought it was safe, he got on the move only to hear the sound again. He kept expecting the black bear and her

Delivering Bad News in Good Ways:
Turn difficult conversations into purposeful dialogue, positive outcomes, & focused results in 3 easy steps

| 135 |

cub to overtake him, but suddenly he was on them.

But here is the twist. It was not a bear but a pig!

This area was new to Peter. He studied the region's wildlife and foliage, and when he learned there were black bears in the area, he was surprised. Black bears, he had read, are usually not aggressive, except when it comes to protecting their cubs.

When Peter saw what he thought was a cub and her mother, his already primed mind made a leap based on what he thought his ears and eyes had confirmed.

He built a whole story around his explanation of the situation. What he learned from his research and interviews of others and his belief in the reliability of his thinking cost him time and physical and emotional stress.

CONFIRMATION BIAS

This is an example of what psychologists call confirmation bias. Things like this give our brain structure and order, which reduces anxiety (or increases it as in Blaber's case!). This is a good example of System 1 thinking in play.

It is not a bad thing to have mental models because they help us function and interact with others. Mental models can also serve as sources of inspiration for creative and innovative endeavors. It offers shortcuts to problem solving. An important step in this process as Tetlock and Gardner say in their book, but it should include a healthy dose of doubt.

Okay, so let me make the point AGAIN that I made earlier in this chapter:

Don't make your first assumption your conclusion

This is why the Evaluate step is so critical. The rush to move on a hunch can result in treating the symptoms, not the problem or it can lead us to an

| 136 |

Delivering Bad News in Good Ways:
Turn difficult conversations into purposeful dialogue, positive outcomes, & focused results in 3 easy steps

altogether wrong answer or solution.

We do sometimes get lucky with our hunches, but it is a slippery slope to believe that will always be the case.

Intuition works if valid information has been integrated into our thinking process. This integration emerges in the form of patterns. Steve Jobs of Apple was famous for "connecting the dots." He used his multi-disciplinary knowledge, experience, observations, and interactions with others to see things in new ways.

Past learning, continued study, facts, and healthy dose of doubt that promote curiosity and questions are important to the Evaluation process. The key to this step is not making your first assumption your conclusion.

Taking the time to step back from the situation and evaluate it objectively sets you up for the final step in the SED Method: Deliver.

Completing the Evaluate step gives us the strategy clarity needed to move on to Delivery. It is the path of least resistance that gets us to the next task quickly.

Just consider, however, the impact of a succession of these snap decisions. If they are anything like the bat and ball problem, we will have a trail of wrong answers that cumulatively create big problems.

In some aspects of work, we have checks and balances to help avoid relying solely on System 1 thinking. Consider these examples:

- Checklist for a pilot landing a plane at O'Hare Airport

- Safety protocols for a journeyman working in a rural part of Pennsylvania

- Procedures for a medical team to use when a victim of a major car accident arrives at the ER of Cedars-Sinai Medical Center in Los Angeles

When it comes to communicating bad news, we are typically left to our own devices. But that is why you're reading this book! You are getting a guide much like the examples above to help manage the situation.

Now it is time to prepare to Deliver the news.

Delivering Bad News in Good Ways:
Turn difficult conversations into purposeful dialogue, positive outcomes, & focused results in 3 easy steps

| 137 |

CHAPTER TAKEAWAYS

▶ Monkey Mind & Storytelling

▶ Reflecting on thoughts and feelings

▶ Reflection to Insight - connecting the dots

▶ Clarify the problem/opportunity

▶ Interpretive questions

▶ System 1 and System 2 thinking

▶ Confirmation bias

▶ Don't make your first assumption your conclusion

| 138 |

Delivering Bad News in Good Ways:
Turn difficult conversations into purposeful dialogue, positive outcomes, & focused results in 3 easy steps

CHAPTER 7:

DELIVER STEP OF THE SED METHOD

CRAFT THE STATEMENT WITH AN EYE TO THE RECEIVER

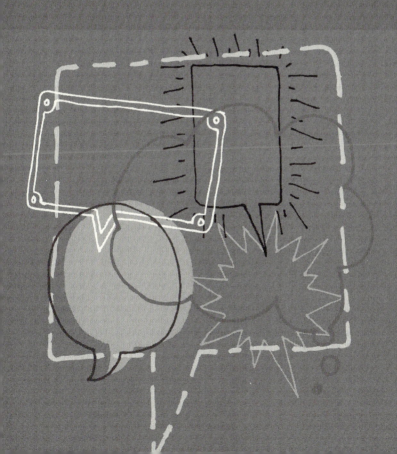

TRANSFORMING THE "MOM" JEAN TO THE "WOW" JEAN

In 2008 VF Corp.—the maker of Lee, Wrangler, Nautica, North Face, Vans and more than 20 other apparel brands and headquartered in Greensboro, NC, USA—had a problem.

That year, the company experienced a five percent revenue decline. Recognizing they needed help, they turned to Innosight, a consulting firm co-founded by Clay Christensen that helps organizations create sustainable growth through innovation. VF and Innosight partnered to create a growth strategy to meet ambitious goals for their Jeanswear division.

Two of VF's flagship brands, Lee® and Riders® by Lee, have long defined comfort and style in jeans. But sales were lagging, with Lee dropping to No. 4 in market share. In March 2009 they kicked off a 10-month project to turn the 'mom' jean into the 'wow' jean.

Lee needed to find a way to regain an edge. Part of the problem was that many women partial to the Lee brand were turned off by the jean shopping experience and had not updated their jeans in years.

A mock commercial on *Saturday Night Live* poked at this phenomenon. Sporting "Mom Jeans" with super high waists, Tina Fey, Amy Poehler, and friends go about gardening and packing kids into mini-vans while oblivious to the fact that their jeans are out of step with the times.

Lee needed to "turn the mom jean into the wow jean" by designing a stylish jean with a delightful fit and at the same time transform the shopping process into more satisfying and effective experience.

One of the issues customers faced was the outdated shopping system. Innosight helped Lee develop a new concept to address these problems: the Riders By Lee Shape System. The new retail system helped women better identify the right jeans by using pictorial descriptions of body types that ranged from curvy to straight.

This new system helped them identify the style that worked best with their body type. It saved time and improved the overall shopping experience because they took fewer pairs of jeans into the fitting room and were able to find a pair that fit well faster.

| 140 |

Delivering Bad News in Good Ways:
Turn difficult conversations into purposeful dialogue, positive outcomes, & focused results in 3 easy steps

To VF Corporation's delight, the new system helped turn around lagging sales.

Following the launch of the new system, the jeans division realized a $100 million gain in revenue. This catapulted Lee to No. 1 in market share in the 30- to 50-year-old female demographic.

Within two years of this project, VF was on a sustained path of double-digit revenue growth across all business units. In 2011 VF Corporation entered the Top 100 on the Barron's 500.

Strong growth of sales and profits as well as return on investment earned them this position for the first time in the company's history. By 2014, VF Corporation moved into the Top 15 on Barron's list among all publicly traded companies in America.

Delivering Bad News in Good Ways:
Turn difficult conversations into purposeful dialogue, positive outcomes, & focused results in 3 easy steps

141

EVALUATE TO DELIVERY: KNOW YOUR TARGET AUDIENCE

*"Your **audience** gives you everything you need. They tell you. There is no director who can direct you like an **audience**." ~ Fanny Brice*

As illustrated in the VF Corporation/Innosight project story, communication with your target market is critical to success. They determine one reason sales declined was because of the outdated shopping experience. The image-driven experience became a new way to communicate with customers.

It is the same with delivering bad news. You might have great content, but the entire thing can flop if you do not have an effective way to communicate with the recipient.

This requires a little assessment and preparation, which we will cover in this chapter.

You have come a long way in the preparation process and now the finish line is in sight. Let's review your accomplishments:

SEPARATE STEP OF THE SED

▶ You gathered information through questions, interviews, and reviews

▶ You parsed fact from opinion

EVALUATE STEP OF THE SED

▶ You assessed your thoughts and feelings

▶ You considered the thoughts and feelings of others

▶ You clarified the problem/opportunity

Now you are ready dive into the **DELIVER,** which is the third and final step of the SED Method.

The Deliver step guides us through preparing to deliver the bad news to the recipient(s). Preparation is critical to facilitating the conversation, or Talk, as you well see in Chapter 8.

| 142 |

Delivering Bad News in Good Ways:
Turn difficult conversations into purposeful dialogue, positive outcomes, & focused results in 3 easy steps

Following a process will help you manage the feelings you have about the situation as well as the things you identified in Chapter 6 that could get in your way. It also helps you anticipate how the receiver may feel and what they may say in response.

It is normal at this point to have a good amount of information on hand. This might feel a bit overwhelming so we are going to spend some time considering how to organize it quickly.

A big part of the Deliver step preparation is mining the information you identified and organized in the previous two steps. To do this, we are going to use grouping and questions to organize and refine what you are going to say, how you are going to say it, and what to do once you have said it.

This is at the heart of the Deliver step of the SED. It is here that we will take what you have done and decide the best way to say and present it.

Our goal is to craft the statement to deliver the bad news in a way that does not shut the receiver down but rather creates dialogue that leads to purposeful next steps.

CRAFTING YOUR STATEMENT

Defining the situation involves sorting the information you gathered during the Separate step of the SED method. You have already done this, so you are ahead of the game!

Remember the example in Chapter 5 of the driver cutting you off in traffic? You will recall that this System 1 inspired equation, **Event Experience + Response = REACT,** describes your brain's natural tendency to draw a quick conclusion before you have had time to truly consider all the facts and possibilities.

In crisis situations, this is not a bad thing. As we established in an earlier chapter, muscle memory gets flexed in a crisis and gives you what you need to respond quickly when a situation is potentially life threatening.

As we know in non-threatening situations, however, it can be more effective to do the following: **Event Experience + Assess + Select = ACT.** Slowing down to assess the situation is useful in moving on to the next step.

Delivering Bad News in Good Ways:
Turn difficult conversations into purposeful dialogue, positive outcomes, & focused results in 3 easy steps

| 143 |

Next we need to pull in your thoughts in the Evaluate step of the SED method. It is here that we have a second shot at assessing our thinking in an effort to uncover blind spots missed the first time around.

Remember Irina in Chapter 6? Her startup suffered a cash crunch, twice. Her company benefited from her ability to hold off action until she was sure she had all the information she needed, partly by following these steps:

- Assessing her thoughts and feelings – emotion, attitude, triggers

- Anticipating team thoughts and feelings – emotion, impact, response

- Impact on the work – time, cost, scope

- Options based on scenario modeling

Irina followed the central point of Chapter 6: **Don't make your first assumption your conclusion.** That is how she set herself up for the third step of SED: Deliver.

One more thing before we consider the Deliver step. Remember those reflective questions? Let's revisit them. Your response to them is critical here.

Some of your responses will serve as a backdrop or reference while you are in the conversation. Other responses will feed directly into the statement you create to start the conversation.

- What is the best you can hope for?
- What is the least you can live with?
- What are your options given the information on hand?
- Anyone you should consult to provide additional perspective?
- Given what you know now, what recommendations can you offer?

The output from the questions above will give you the foundation for the focus of your delivery.

The content of bad news delivery obviously is important, but there is another part that needs attention. While the content of your message provides the "what," it does not speak to the "how."

It is the "how" that ensures the "what" is heard and understood.

| 144 |

Delivering Bad News in Good Ways:
Turn difficult conversations into purposeful dialogue, positive outcomes, & focused results in 3 easy steps

DELIVER – STOP PRESENTING TO YOURSELF!

When tasked with delivering bad news, we are often so focused on the content that we treat too lightly or skip altogether how we are going to say it.

When we present, we tend to present in a way that is most comfortable to us instead of considering how to present in a way that the receiver relates and connects. I learned this lesson many years ago when I was working with a tech startup in Canada.

I tend to go deep with assignments to the point that my colleagues at that company dubbed me "The Investigator." I love research and equally love sharing it. When I had to present my findings, however, I invariably lost my audience. It puzzled me.

The information was solid and very appropriate to the task, but people tended to fade on me halfway through my presentations. At first I thought they just did not have time to pay attention, and then it occurred to me: *I might be the problem.*

So, true to form, I researched it. And I watched my colleagues. I know that sounds a wee creepy, but it was in the spirit of learning what they responded to and what engaged them.

My one boss, Karla Stephens-Tolstoy, the CEO and co-founder of the company, had a strong marketing background and was very charismatic and visual. My other boss, Regina Miller, COO and co-founder of the company, was a storyteller and gifted experience designer. They both loved team brainstorming and coming up with ideas in the moment.

As you can imagine with two bosses with skills and preferences like that, I had my work cut out for me.

To date my presentations were the opposite of what they found interesting and stimulating. My slideshows were filled with facts, tables, numbers, and no images. I did not have any anchor information to guide the conversation.

I began to understand that my lack of effectiveness was because I was essentially presenting to myself!

Delivering Bad News in Good Ways:
Turn difficult conversations into purposeful dialogue, positive outcomes, & focused results in 3 easy steps

| 145

I presented information in a way that I preferred – not in the way my audience needed it to truly hear and engage. They were drowning in my ocean of information. No wonder they drifted during my presentations!

I interviewed key decision makers to understand their preferences. I dove into research about persuasion and decision making styles.

It was clear that Karla, the sponsor of many of my presentations, had a Charismatic style, which we will cover later in this chapter. She needed brevity, few facts, powerful visuals, and lots of time for discussion and brainstorming.

It was on me to stretch way outside my comfort zone in an effort to help others connect with the information in ways that were familiar to the team.

It was then that my presentation delivery underwent a metamorphosis. Once I understood what needed to change, I went to work reconfiguring the next presentation so it suited the style of the primary decision maker, who in this case was the CEO.

The big day came. I kept the slides to a minimum. The recommendation options (three) were at the beginning of the presentation followed by supporting evidence. There were a ton of images to help tell the story of the findings and recommendations.

At the end of the presentation I noted all the links to the documentation would be sent out after the meeting, which satisfied my "Thinker" style preference. More about that in the next section.

There was no drifting off. People asked questions. There was plenty of time for discussion and brainstorming. The post presentation consensus was positive.

Whew!

Although it was tough to go through that, I am eternally grateful for the patience of the team. It was a growth moment and a process I can share with you here so you will not have to suffer like I did.

| 146 |

Delivering Bad News in Good Ways:
Turn difficult conversations into purposeful dialogue, positive outcomes, & focused results in 3 easy steps

STYLE AND METHOD MATTER

In their consulting practice, Gary A. Williams and Robert B. Miller made an interesting observation. When attempting to persuade decision-makers, if the person focused too much on the content of their augment and not enough on the delivery, their chances of success decreased.

This often left the presenter wondering what went wrong as it did me in the previous story. Williams and Miller decided to try to find out what was behind the decrease.

They and their team spent two years surveying and interpreting the results gathered from nearly 1,700 executives in a wide range of industries. The results of their research were published in article titled *"Change the Way You Persuade"* in the **Harvard Business Review,** May 2002.

Concluding that we have a tendency to focus on the **content** of the message and far less time on **how** the message is delivered, Williams and Miller identified five decision-making styles that can be used as a guide for persuading others.

Let's look at how to use those styles to determine the best way to deliver bad news.

Delivering Bad News in Good Ways:
Turn difficult conversations into purposeful dialogue, positive outcomes, & focused results in 3 easy steps

147

DETERMINE THE RECEIVER'S STYLE AND APPROACH

Now that we have had a chance to separate and evaluate the situation, it is time to round out the plan with how we need to deliver the news to the recipient. Notice I did not say how we "want" to deliver.

It is a subtle but important distinction. This small distinction can make a big difference in how the receiver responds to the news.

Tailoring the message to that person's **decision-making style** will go a long way to deliver bad news in a way that can be heard by the intended receiver.

Delivering bad news in the most effective way means assessing the receiver's preferences first.

Consider the following:

▶ What drives or influences them

▶ What information do they need and in what context

▶ When should you tell them and how long do they need to consider the information

▶ How should the information be structured

▶ What medium or materials are best

Let's return to Williams and Miller's model as laid out in their *Harvard Business Review* article.

Before determining the best way to open the discussion, the materials you will need, and the timing, consider which of the following styles best represents your recipient's style.

DECISION-MAKING STYLE: FOLLOWERS
36% OF DECISION-MAKERS

Make decisions based on how other trusted decision-makers or they have made similar decisions in the past.

| 148 |

Delivering Bad News in Good Ways:
Turn difficult conversations into purposeful dialogue, positive outcomes, & focused results in 3 easy steps

Responsible, cautious, and bargain conscious. Usually risk-averse.

Need to see that it has been somehow done before.

Your MO: Focus on proven methods and testimonials.

Examples: Peter Coors of Coors Beer and Carly Fiorina, former Hewlett-Packard CEO

DECISION-MAKING STYLE: CHARISMATIC
25% OF DECISION-MAKERS

Tends to be exuberant about a new idea or proposal. Final decision is based on balanced information, not just emotions.

Captivating, enthusiastic, dominant, and talkative. Seeks out risk.

Uses simple, straightforward arguments and visual aids.

Your MO: Resist the temptation to jump on this style's bandwagon of initial excitement.

Examples: Richard Branson of Virgin corporation and Oprah Winfrey, entertainment and production mogul

DECISION-MAKING STYLE: SKEPTICS
19% OF DECISION-MAKERS

Highly suspicious of data that do not fit with or challenge their worldview.

Make decisions based on their gut feelings.

Combative style, usually described as take-charge individuals.

Demanding, disruptive, rebellious.

Your MO: Establish as much credibility and clout as possible with this person. Get support from someone whom this decision-maker trusts before delivery.

Examples: Larry Ellison of Oracle and Steve Case of America Online

Delivering Bad News in Good Ways:
Turn difficult conversations into purposeful dialogue, positive outcomes, & focused results in 3 easy steps

| 149 |

DECISION-MAKING STYLE: THINKERS
11% OF DECISION-MAKERS

Impressed with data. Can exhibit contradictory points of view within a single meeting.

Need to cautiously work through all options before making a decision. Can be the toughest to persuade and are risk averse.

Logical and academic.

Your MO: Have lots of data available. They need as much info as possible to make a decision.

Examples: Bill Gates of Microsoft and Alan Greenspan, former chairman of the U.S. Federal Reserve (1987-2006)

DECISION-MAKING STYLE: CONTROLLERS
9% OF DECISION-MAKERS

Hate ambiguity.

Focus on the pure facts and analytics of a decision because of their own fears and uncertainties.

Tend to be logical, unemotional, detail-oriented, and analytical.

Risk-averse.

Your MO: Do not be too aggressive. Present the facts and details and leave it to the decision maker to work through.

Examples: Martha Stewart of Martha Stewart Omnimedia and American businessman Ross Perot

▶ CONSIDER YOUR PRIMARY RECEIVER

▶ What is their style?

▶ How do you know?

▶ If you are not sure, whom can you ask for an opinion?

▶ What do you need to do to prepare your materials and information?

▶ **TWO BIGGEST MISTAKES PEOPLE MAKE WITH DELIVERING BAD NEWS**

1. They focus on the content and not the delivery, using a one-size-fits-all approach.

2. They present in their own preferred style, rather than to the style of the person receiving the news. They have preconceived ideas about how the recipient will respond.

Most people tailor the message toward **Thinkers** and **Controllers,** which make up the smallest population of the five styles.

▶ **IN DELIVERING BAD NEWS, THERE ARE SIX BEST PRACTICES TO FOLLOW:**

1. Take time to plan but do not use that as an excuse to put off doing it.

2. Craft your pitch to the primary recipient style.

3. Do it live, either in person or video/audio chat.

4. Be open and honest. Tell the truth.

5. Give the facts first, then opinion.

6. Be brief. Draft key points to stay on track.

7. Give the recipient time. You have had time with the news already; they need time, too.

From a logical, rational standpoint these steps look easy, right? Sure...follow the process and you will have no problem with delivery.

Okay, that is your cortical brain talking to you. It is happy to tell you in its very rational, logical voice that such things are a piece of cake. But then there is our sneaky, ever relentless limbic or "feeling brain" tugging at us. It is sending you overt physical clues that it is not as straightforward as your rational self claims.

It is the part that turns on the sweat gland faucet, marshals the butterflies in your stomach to start flapping, and commands your hands to move or tremble as if they have a will of their own.

This can set off a chain of events that may lead you to fumble, tumble, and fall through what should be an easy process, according to the previously noted steps.

Delivering Bad News in Good Ways:
Turn difficult conversations into purposeful dialogue, positive outcomes, & focused results in 3 easy steps

| 151 |

Before you know it, your emotional self makes clear who is truly in charge and you find yourself figuratively on the floor as the receiver flattens you further with every soul-crushing stomped response.

Okay, well, that is definitely no fun.

So let's pick you up off the floor, let gravity fill in the voids (whether you want it to or not), and start over.

This time let's do a bit more advance work so you can avoid ending up a pancake the next time round.

| 152 |

Delivering Bad News in Good Ways:
Turn difficult conversations into purposeful dialogue, positive outcomes, & focused results in 3 easy steps

DO THE ADVANCE WORK

How you prepare for the conversation is critically important. Let's review the five steps for success inspired by Natalie Cooper, who is noted in Paul B. Brown's *NY Times* 2008 article *Finding the Best Ways to Break Bad News:*

1. Prepare bullet points or a script to ensure a consistent message
2. Identify the location and timing
3. Pick your bearer
4. Consider and plan delivery
5. Follow the steps in Chapter 8 to help guide the conversation after you deliver the news

Tip No. 1 is reinforced by Susan Berkley, author of **The Voice Coach** and also noted in Brown's article. Her suggestions inspired the list below.

▶ Separate the people from the problem.

▶ Give all the facts and be truthful.

▶ Let recipients of bad news get it out. Negative emotions must be dealt with before taking action.

▶ It is insensitive to tell stakeholders not to worry or be angry. Empathy is important here.

▶ Outline a specific plan of action even if it is just brainstorming next steps.

▶ Do not make promises you cannot keep. Do what you say you are going to do.

Where and when you deliver bad news has an impact on the recipient, which is why Tip No. 2 is so important. Always deliver bad news in person. Doing it by phone is bad; it is even worse by text or email. You owe it to your team, a vendor, your manager, or an investor to look them in the eye when you have bad news to share.

Depending on the situation, the location of the conversation can affect the success or failure your delivery. If possible, share bad news in a neutral location and eliminate physical barriers between you and the recipient. The better you are at creating a "we're all in this together" environment, the more open the receiver will be.

Delivering Bad News in Good Ways:
Turn difficult conversations into purposeful dialogue, positive outcomes, & focused results in 3 easy steps

| 153 |

Delivering bad news can be emotional for you and your audience. For this reason alone, do not "wing it." Your relationship with the other person, your internal needs and values, and the impact of your news on the other person can influence how you feel during the process.

A script will help to ensure that you will deliver a consistent message (Tip No. 3).

Dr. Robert Buckman was a cancer specialist who taught doctors and consulted with Fortune 500 companies. Before his death in 2011, he helped other physicians with the difficult task of delivering what could be the worst news their patients would ever receive: they had cancer.

For Tip No. 4, consider his thoughts on how to deliver bad news in good ways:

▶ Begin a difficult conversation by listening.

▶ State the news plainly and give the recipient a chance to absorb what they have heard.

▶ Give the other person time – silence is okay.

▶ End by summarizing. Review the ground you've covered, identify a plan, agree on a 'contract' for the next contact.

▶ Practice if it makes you feel more comfortable.

▶ Take notes into the meeting.

▶ Start with open-ended questions.

▶ Explore perceptions before you try to define reality.

Dr. Buckman also thought it is important to use open-ended questions to encourage a response beyond yes, no, or maybe. This creates opportunity for dialogue. It also helps establish trust.

The way people hear the bad news (or rather what you might think is bad news if it were told to you) might not be perceived the way you anticipate.

Be careful of inserting your own opinion into the conversation. We all tend to go into conversations with preconceived ideas and assumptions based on past experiences. This can help you and others from getting emotional.

| 154 |

Delivering Bad News in Good Ways:
Turn difficult conversations into purposeful dialogue, positive outcomes, & focused results in 3 easy steps

Now that you have scripted an honest and open message and thought about when and where to deliver it, it is time to consider whether you are the best messenger. It is best to have someone who is careful, considerate, *and* has the authority to act to handle the conversation.

PICKING THE MESSENGER

You are reading this book to learn how to be that person. But if you have not had enough practice yet, and you are worried about your ability to pull it off, consider asking someone else in the company, perhaps another manager familiar with your project, to take the reins.

Watch and listen carefully and learn for the next time.

Finally, consider and plan the delivery. If you are not going to be the messenger, work closely with the person who will be.

Craft a brief and direct statement. Think through the approach. Develop an outline or draw pictures, whatever you think will help. Be objective. When it is time to share the news, be timely, factual, and clear.

Once you have opened the discussion, the goal is to collaborate on the next steps. In **Chapter 8**, we will consider that process.

CHAPTER TAKEAWAYS

▶ Present to the receiver's style, not yourself

▶ Tips for how to craft the statement

▶ Determine materials needed — best way them to hear it

▶ Identify the location and timing

▶ Considerations for delivery

◆

Delivering Bad News in Good Ways:
Turn difficult conversations into purposeful dialogue, positive outcomes, & focused results in 3 easy steps

| 155 |

CHAPTER 8:

AFTER SED - NOW WHAT?

LET'S TALK IT OUT

POP GOES THE BUBBLE

It was early 2002, and the privately owned mortgage business with offices throughout the southeastern region of the United States was growing at a staggering annual rate of 10 percent. The nation was emerging from a devastating tech bubble, so some good news in any sector was more than welcome.

Ian, the CEO, carefully watched the housing sector, which was on track to hit a 40-year high of over 6 percent of Real GDP by 2005. With this kind of growth, Ian easily saw outside investment was needed for badly needed capital to keep pace with the anticipated growth of the industry.

Ian and his leadership team worked diligently for months to find the right investment partner. It wasn't hard. Clearly, this was a hot sector and plenty of people were lining up to get in on the action.

After several meetings over many months, Mac, a self-proclaimed simple country farmer, ponied up a several million-dollar investment for Ian's business. Mac owned agricultural enterprises across the US.

As an "ag and land man" Mac believed deeply in land and home ownership. While he didn't know the mortgage business, he trusted people will always need a place to live, and so this was a smart investment with an even smarter team.

Thanks to Mac's investment, Ian and his team were able to grow the firm at a rate that outpaced their competitors. The firm's reputation for fairness was helping in its quest for market share. Chatter increased about expanding beyond the southeast by issuing franchise licenses. People were asking for it already. The firm was riding high.

Over the next few years they expanded their adjustable rate mortgage division, building solid relationships with numerous lending institutions. The company's reputation strengthened further as the group began to take on hard-to-fund loans. Because of their relationships, they could get just about anyone approved.

Delivering Bad News in Good Ways:
Turn difficult conversations into purposeful dialogue, positive outcomes, & focused results in 3 easy steps

| 157 |

In the meantime, Ian began to catch articles here and there from prominent financial publications hinting that there might be trouble brewing in the lending and housing paradise. While Ian kept these warnings in the periphery, he moved forward with the company's expansion, hiring more people and making infrastructure purchases.

By 2006 home prices began a steady decline, which made it more difficult for borrowers to refinance their loans. In the meantime, many of the adjustable-rate mortgages began to reset at higher interest rates, which resulted in higher monthly payments. This caused mortgage delinquencies to soar. Ian didn't know it yet, but the worst was yet to come.

Ian and his team took stock of the situation. Erring on the side of caution, they began to dial back the expansion plans and tighten spending. For a while it seemed this would be enough, but month over month revenue continued to drop with mortgage requests drying up and lending getting harder. If his business was going to survive, Ian needed help.

It was time to talk to Mac.

Ian planned carefully for the meeting. He knew it was going to be tough because of how well they had been doing for the past several years.

This was likely going to be a shock to Mac, who believed unfailingly in the power of land and home ownership – "Everybody needs a place to live so this business is a no-brainer. It's foolish not to place your bet on a sure thing!" Mac passionately declared during their state of the company review in the previous year.

Ian dreaded the conversation. Everything had taken an incredible nosedive so fast. He had little feeling for how Mac might respond. Ian pulled together a few simple charts because Mac was a self-described "picture" guy. "Talk simple to me," he'd often tell Ian with a wink.

He chose to meet Mac at his office. Ian thought Mac would feel more comfortable hearing the bad news on his own turf.

Ian opened the meeting with a simple statement to get the conversation started.

| 158 |

Delivering Bad News in Good Ways:
Turn difficult conversations into purposeful dialogue, positive outcomes, & focused results in 3 easy steps

"Mac, quarter over quarter since your initial investment the firm has experienced tremendous growth. In the last three quarters, however, we have witnessed a dramatic drop in revenue. Have you been keeping up with the news lately in the lending space?"

"Not really," he said with only a slight hint of concern.

"Well, there appears to be an issue brewing that suggests the lending and housing market is in the process of taking a significant downturn. We have dialed back expansion plans and tightened our budget, but we may need additional capital to shore up the business in case the downturn is protracted. With the cuts and changes we have made, we think we can weather this storm, but we'll need some help."

"How much?" Mac asked, with his face slackening.

"One million dollars will give us a sizeable length of runway."

Mac thought for a few minutes. "That's a lot of money right now. I'm starting to feel a little squeeze with my ag ventures. It seems housing is not the only area feeling a pinch."

That opening exchange kicked off a deep, long discussion about Mac's constraints and Ian's concerns. Mac said $1 million was too rich for him right now, but he could do something. They went back and forth on the amount and what Ian could do to readjust his plan to match Mac's capability.

It took a while, but they landed on a solution that worked for both of them. Ian reviewed the takeaways with Mac and then returned to the firm to inform the team.

The firm was lucky it had such a savvy CEO. Ian paid attention to the hints in the media and chatter among his financial network.

Unlike others, he jumped on shoring up his business well before the "housing bubble" burst in 2007, which kicked off a much longer period of stagnation than Ian originally thought. It was tough going, but the firm survived — although as a shadow of its former self.

Delivering Bad News in Good Ways:
Turn difficult conversations into purposeful dialogue, positive outcomes, & focused results in 3 easy steps

| 159 |

Ian later admitted he had been tempted to continue to ride the "gravy train" all the way to the housing train wreck, but he resisted the "too good to be true" temptation, bit the bullet, and tackled the bad news of the reality sooner than later.

160

Delivering Bad News in Good Ways:
Turn difficult conversations into purposeful dialogue, positive outcomes, & focused results in 3 easy steps

BE AN IAN

Ian did not know it at the time, but the world was about to enter one of the most critically debilitating times in modern history. Household debt expansion was financed with mortgage-backed securities (MBS) and collateralized debt obligations (CDO).

In the beginning this type of backing offered attractive rates of return due to the higher interest rates on mortgages, but unfortunately many lower credit quality borrowers, who could not afford the mortgages after the adjustable rate came to term, caused massive mortgage defaults. As a result, the U.S. entered a deep recession, with nearly 9 million jobs lost during 2008 and 2009 and housing prices falling nearly 30 percent.

Ian did not have a crystal ball, but he did have an objective eye that helped him save his business when others failed.

Let's look at what he did (and did not do).

▶ Did not fall prey to temporal discounting

▶ Ignored confirmation bias

▶ Assessed the facts

▶ Evaluated the options

▶ Prepared for the discussion

▶ Presented the bad news to Mac in a way that Mac preferred

▶ Discussed the situation and settled on a plan

You can see the SED Method steps in his actions.

What we have not covered is THE TALK – what do you do once you are in the conversation with the person (or people) to whom you deliver the bad news?

Let's find out...

Delivering Bad News in Good Ways:
Turn difficult conversations into purposeful dialogue, positive outcomes, & focused results in 3 easy steps

| 161 |

WHERE TO GO FROM HERE

Congratulations! Like Ian, you know how to do the following:

▸ Gather facts and opinions of the situation (Chapter 5)

▸ Evaluate your feelings, assess the possible feeling of others, and identify options (Chapter 6)

▸ Determine how best to present the news in a way that can be heard (Chapter 7)

But what do you do once you are in the conversation?

While there are many good resources to help you for the actual conversation, we will touch on a typical process to round out your experience with this book. Additional resources can be found at my website at *www.alisonsigmon. com/books/resources.*

BEGIN WITH THE OPENING STATEMENT – THE TALK

As noted in Chapter 7, the discussion should begin with the opening statement. The news likely requires some discussion and action, which we will get to a little deeper in this chapter.

Depending on the gravity of the news, the person may need time to process what you have shared. Remember like we considered with Anvi's situation in Chapter 4, you have had time with the information, but the recipient has not – they are likely hearing it for the first time. Giving pause and silence are important at this point.

You have already identified ways they may respond when you moved through the Evaluation step in Chapter 6. Our inclination especially in stressful conversations is to fill the void of silence. Simply wait. Breathe deeply and gently as the person (people?) absorb the news. Once they appear ready or they tell you they are ready to continue, you can begin.

Our goals are purposeful dialogue, positive outcomes, and focused results. Considering that you are delivering bad news, this might seem impossible. Following a simple process while in the midst of the discussion will go a long way to achieving it.

Borrowing from parts of the *Harvard Business Negotiation Study* and from a negotiation model created by my mentor, Jan Renerts Newton, I offer you a simple follow on process to the **SED method** that we can call the **Talk.** There are three steps:

1. Agree on the problem or challenge

2. Determine a solution with consideration for both parties

3. Identify authority and next steps

Let's break it down...

1: AGREE ON THE PROBLEM OR CHALLENGE

In Chapter 5 we introduced objective questions from the ORID model. You used them for your own understanding and subsequent analysis of the situation. So, in the spirit of NOT reinventing the wheel, you can use them during your conversation with the receiver in an effort to glean facts, better understand their perspective, and identify the issues.

This first step of the **Talk** is all about actively listening and asking questions. Active listening is about being present and focused on the conversation. It means NOT multi-tasking. It is an opportunity to get the other person's perspective and "walk a mile in their shoes" on the journey to creating positive outcomes from the bad news.

This step, for me, is like partnering to solve a puzzle or to participate in a treasure hunt that requires solving clues and sharing information. It requires asking questions, assessing the information, and eliminating the distractions (things not relevant to the current situation).

As you ask questions, mentally check their body language to avoid lingering in the question asking stage too long. For further information on body language, please check out resources I have put together for you on the subject at *www.alisonsigmon.com/books/resources.*

Be sure to paraphrase what you think you have heard them say. Ask for confirmation so you can add your thoughts to theirs if you think it is appropriate.

Delivering Bad News in Good Ways:
Turn difficult conversations into purposeful dialogue, positive outcomes, & focused results in 3 easy steps

| 163 |

These are good steps in the active listening process. There are great resources for active listening, which we will not rehash here. If you are interested in additional resources you can find them on the Internet or at my website *www.alisonsigmon.com/books/resources.*

It is tempting to jump to a solution before the situation is fully understood. This kind of conversation can be stressful, which means we will likely be eager to be done with it as soon as possible. Resist that temptation. Before moving on, summarize your understanding of the issue and ensure the person (or people) are in agreement with that summary.

Asking questions, paraphrasing, and agreeing on the problem or challenge relative to the bad news is the first step in the dialogue process, but what is dialogue?

According to William Isaacs in his book **Dialogue and the Art of Thinking Together,** dialogue is a conversation with a center, not sides. He continues with the following:

"It is a way of taking the energy of our differences and channeling it toward something that has never been created before. It lifts us out of polarization and into a greater common sense...dialogue is a conversation in which people think together in relationship. Thinking together implies that you no longer take your own position as final. You relax your grip on certainty and listen to possibilities that result simply from being in relationship with others' possibilities that might not otherwise have occurred."

And yet, William Isaacs continues with making the point that when in a conversation, *"People don't listen, they reload."*

So, what gets in the way of dialogue?

► Preconceived ideas

► Expectations for how the conversation should go

► Filters (Thinking Process in Chapter 5)

► Assumptions (storytelling!)

► Cultural misunderstanding

- Overanalyzing the situation

- Lack of understanding of the issue

- Past experience with the person (baggage)

- Unknown influences (their boss perhaps?)

- Letting go of our own needs

- Polarized thinking (it can only be my way - remember Ellis in Chapter 3)

If you think something is getting in the way of effective dialogue then assess your options:

- Considerately share that you are feeling stalled, stuck, or whatever appropriate word describes how you are feeling and ask for their help

- Take a break from it and circle back

- Suggest inviting another person to join the conversation

- What else comes to mind for you?

Time consideration and urgency will drive your actions in this case. In the Anvi example from Chapter 4, she decided she had the time to give the team to process the news so they broke for the day and circled back to the situation the following day. This is not always possible, but you can work with the receiver of the bad news to determine if it is necessary.

Let's consider some research that reinforces the importance of purposeful work and the emotional investment given to it. It is this deep investment that supports the need for giving time to the recipient of the bad news.

Basically, they need time to grieve the loss when something on which they worked so hard is taken away or underappreciated.

Delivering Bad News in Good Ways:
Turn difficult conversations into purposeful dialogue, positive outcomes, & focused results in 3 easy steps

| 165 |

MORE THAN JUST TOYS

In his Ted Talk titled *What makes us feel good about our work?*, Dan Ariely, a behavioral economist, notes that he and his colleagues completed a series of experiments to assess how the perceived purpose of tasks influenced a person's willingness to work.

In one of the experiments, participants in the first group were paid a small fee to assemble a Lego Bionicle toy, and when they completed the task, it was displayed.

Each building round, the amount they would be paid for building the toy was reduced by ten cents, but each completed toy was displayed while participants worked on more.

The second group was given the same opportunity for the same paid amount. What was different with the second group was that when the participant completed building the toy, the researcher dismantled it in front of them as they were building a new toy.

The first group built far more toys than the second group. Why? Because they felt a sense of purpose. Seeing their work on display made them feel there was value in their effort. The second group, on the other hand, quickly felt the meaninglessness of their task and abandoned it.

This experiment demonstrates that when people feel a sense of purpose, they feel an emotional connection and responsibility for that work. They will work long hours, put their personal lives on hold, and put up with outside of the norm requests to meet deadlines, problem solve, and work through issues. They often even do it with a great attitude – they are energetic, engaged, and optimistic.

So, with that understanding, it is easy to see how bad news on a project can temporarily derail a team. If the project is canceled, shifted, shelved, or a proposed solution did not work, there will be an emotional cost and even a lost sense of purpose.

Emotional connection to work and projects is a double-edged sword. As managers of work and projects, we want emotional investment of stakeholders because they will feel more buy-in, commitment, and ownership for the process and outcome.

The truly devoted pour themselves into the work, but if that work is dismantled like the Lego Bionicle toys in Ariely's experiments, then they likely will need some time to recover.

Delivering Bad News in Good Ways:
Turn difficult conversations into purposeful dialogue, positive outcomes, & focused results in 3 easy steps

| 167 |

TRANSITIONING FROM STEP 1 TO STEP 2 OF THE TALK

As noted in the previous section, before moving on to the next step, it is best to summarize the problem/issue that emerged from your dialogue. I like to use visual language to recap. For example, I might say something like the following:

Hareesh, I heard you have not one but two concerns. 1) The budget cut will mean we can't provide the functionality in the project that the client specifically said is a have-to-have; and 2) Not including that client valued functionality might result in the client canceling the project altogether.

This situation is deeply concerning for you since we have had a couple of other performance issues that delayed the timeline earlier in the project, which affected the client's trust in our performance. Further changes may cause more erosion of trust.

To transition in this example, we can tell Hareesh that both are important and ask him which one he thinks is the most critical to address first. This moves us fully into the second step of the Talk.

2: DETERMINE A SOLUTION WITH CONSIDERATION FOR BOTH PARTIES

In this step, we work with the receiver to assess the situation options. Walking into this conversation, you already have an idea of what you would like to do, but because the news impacts the other person, you want to get their voice to the table as well.

Engaging them in this way creates an environment of collaboration, buy-in, and commitment to the positive outcome you are seeking.

To do this we start with asking for ideas on how to address the situation. Ask questions such as the following:

▻ What ideas do you have to address this situation?

▻ Can you imagine what might work?

Listen carefully as they talk for things with which you agree. Take notes if necessary. You do not have to immediately buy into what they suggest the solution should be.

Discuss the pros and cons. Share your ideas on what you think will work. Chances are the solution will sit somewhere between what you want and what they want.

Consider if anyone else needs to be part of the discussion. If you decide more people should be included, or more research needs to be done, then decide who will do what next and when you both will circle back.

If they get off-topic, create a pause with a summary of what has been said so far. You can own the pause as a need for you to take stock of where you both are in the discussion.

For me, this part feels a bit like a dance that starts off uncertain but improves as we better understand the steps or music. This feeling is represented well in music with a term called syncopation.

Often used in jazz, syncopation uses nontraditional beats, which makes the sound seem somewhat disjointed. If your ear can hang in for a bit, syncopation typically transitions and the listener is rewarded with delicious three- or four-count rhythms.

During the second stage, that is often what we are experiencing – disjointed uncertainty. As the conversation continues, understanding will grow for your respective interests. In this step we continue to deepen trust by listening, asking questions, and sharing our thoughts.

Also, use your inner voice to keep reminding yourself to avoid taking things personally in this process. This is not about you or the other person. It's about the issue that sits in between you that require both of you and your respective party of experience (remember Chapter 5!) to address it.

The other person does not have to know this process for it to work. As long as they feel heard and acknowledged, oftentimes they will naturally follow the process and pace you set. Typically the other person or people want to get past the syncopation part as much as you do!

Once you both have landed on a solution to which you can agree, the conversation is ready to transition to the third step: Identify authority and next steps.

Delivering Bad News in Good Ways:
Turn difficult conversations into purposeful dialogue, positive outcomes, & focused results in 3 easy steps

| 169 |

3: IDENTIFY AUTHORITY AND NEXT STEPS

By this point, you both should have a good feel for the solution. Now it is time to determine who will do what and when it will be done. It is tempting to speed through this part, but do not do that.

Being clear about what will happen AFTER the discussion builds in accountability to the results and will make the overall experience more focused and positive.

Once you have decided who will do what, summarize accountabilities and let them know you will follow up with an email. Set a date for the next time you meet if that is appropriate.

| 170 |

Delivering Bad News in Good Ways:
Turn difficult conversations into purposeful dialogue, positive outcomes, & focused results in 3 easy steps

AFTER DELIVERY – FALL OUT

"Words can never adequately convey the incredible impact of our attitudes toward life. The longer I live the more convinced I become that life is 10 percent what happens to us and 90 percent how we respond to it."
~ Charles R. Swindoll

There is never a shortage of challenging situations that result in needing to deliver bad news. Consider these examples:

The marketing strategy you and your team implemented for your company's new, innovative product that, according to consumer research, is going to take the market space by storm is failing and failing badly.

After nearly a year of development on a technical system to integrate several disparate processes within customer service, end user testing results are showing a very low usability and adoption rate.

You've just found out your resources have been slashed by 30 percent, but the sponsor won't budge on the workload. More with less is the mandate.

Once you feel you have a handle on your initial reaction to the news you have just heard, now it is time to assess the intensity and impact.

"Bad news" typically means change for our project, but the purpose of this section is not to rehash the thoughtful models and processes for assessing change and the impact of it. Instead, we will focus on the emotional evaluation and management aspect the change the bad news will likely create.

Delivering Bad News in Good Ways:
Turn difficult conversations into purposeful dialogue, positive outcomes, & focused results in 3 easy steps

| 171 |

TIPS FOR EASING THROUGH THE FALL-OUT

While giving bad news will likely sting on some level no matter how aware and prepared you are, there are a few things you can do to mitigate the situation. Some of these points we covered in Chapter 7, but it is good to revisit them as things to remember while moving through the discussion.

▶ Get a handle on your own emotions by spending time with your response to the bad news first.

▶ What you consider to bad news may not be for the receiver, so check your assumptions.

▶ Plan how and when you are going to share it. Do not avoid or delay. It will only make the situation worse.

▶ Accept you cannot completely change the response of the receiver, but you can definitely influence it through preparation and delivery.

▶ Be direct, focused, and empathetic. Line up the facts. Be prepared to share your position.

▶ Give the receiver time to recover from the news. Their response is more about them and their fear, concern, etc. than it is about you.

▶ Have solution recommendations on hand to facilitate next steps.

▶ Consider what change stage stakeholders may be in, and manage the situation from that model as reviewed in Chapter 4.

Remember, part of your job as a manager delivering bad news is to understand not just the impact on the time, cost, and scope, but also understanding how people feel in response to it.

As previously noted, people move at their own pace when faced with change. A keyword search on change management in amazon.com shows more than 16,000 results! Obviously there is no one right response.

With preparation, understanding, and focus, bad news does not have to be the end of the world, but instead can be an opportunity once the dust settles.

| 172 |

Delivering Bad News in Good Ways:
Turn difficult conversations into purposeful dialogue, positive outcomes, & focused results in 3 easy steps

CHAPTER TAKEAWAYS

▶ Be an Ian

▶ The Talk steps

▶ Tips for managing the conversation and post conversation environment

Delivering Bad News in Good Ways:
Turn difficult conversations into purposeful dialogue, positive outcomes, & focused results in 3 easy steps

| 173 |

CHAPTER 9:
THE END & THE BEGINNING
LOOKING BACK TO MOVE FORWARD

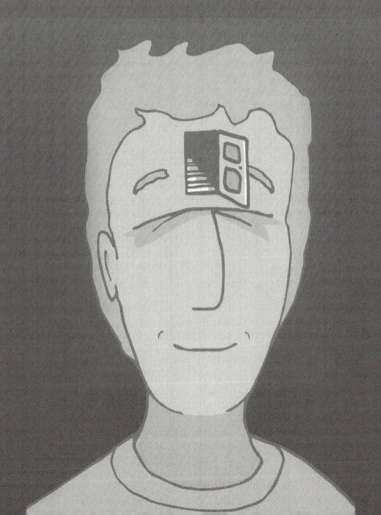

FINALLY! THE END (AND OPPORTUNITY!) ARE HERE

Whew! You have made it to the end. To celebrate your accomplishment, you decide a day at the beach is the perfect way to reflect on what you read in this book and turn it into insights (remember that from Chapter 6?) that you can use in your work and in your life.

So, imagine this…

It is a sunny day. The sky is a stunning, cloudless deep blue. The tide is out and the wind is mild.

You decide on a stroll among the dunes. As the seagrass keeps time with the gentle, steady wind, you pause to watch little fiddler crabs tickle the sand lightly in between skillful bobs above and below the grains. Even with their busy, active pace they never seem to lose sight of the water. Your eyes follow their gaze.

Looking out at the vast, undulating sea, you move to the shoreline where you enjoy the wet, cool sand as it oozes between your toes with each relaxed step.

You haven't a care in the world. The sea is so still you barely hear the waves softly lapping the sand. Seabirds grab your eye as they wheel above pursuing their one truth, which reminds you of Mary Oliver's lovely poem, "The Kingfisher."

Touching an object with the edge of your toes, your attention is pulled down to the ground where you discover a colorful seashell. You reach down to have a closer look when…

BAM! Out of nowhere a wave crashes right where you stand. You're rolling and tumbling beneath the waves, and you quickly realize you are way in over your head.

The water recedes; you manage to catch your breath. You've barely struggled to your knees when a wall of water pushes you forward, and then pulls you back toward the sea. Panicking now, you look for someone to grab your hand and pull you to safety.

Delivering Bad News in Good Ways:
Turn difficult conversations into purposeful dialogue, positive outcomes, & focused results in 3 easy steps

| 175 |

Uh-oh. You've just been hit by bad news.

Even though you know what to do, your reaction is likely to be a visceral one, probably just as physical as emotional in its intensity. You might initially be afraid. Your impulse may be to run away. You may want someone to save you.

In an effort to delay response, you may even play the "what if" game (some call it the "if only" game).

"What if I'd gone to the park today instead of the beach, that wave couldn't have it me." "If only I'd just stayed home and ordered in a pizza. If only..."

When hit with bad news, what is the difference between you and someone who has not read this book? You know these feelings are normal and fleeting. You also know how to deal with them.

As noted in the introduction, we are living in a fast-paced, ever-evolving digital era, which requires nimble, flexible response and rapid change. This change often impacts managers and stakeholders in unpredictable ways. It may even feel like the wave in our story.

In project work, processes help move it through the changes that are inevitable. Technical processes are important to managing time, cost, and scope. Behavioral processes facilitate the interactions and activities needed to achieve the technical process objectives.

As pointed out in the introduction, however, it is the behavioral side of work and projects where we typically hit speed bumps. Why? Because change involves people, and we understand now that comfort with change and our tolerance threshold for change, varies.

As we have established, delivering bad news is rarely our favorite thing to do. Let's return to the questions posed at the beginning of the book:

► **Why** is delivering bad news so hard?

► **What** are the tactics we use to avoid or postpone it?

► **How** do we make it worse by putting it off?

| 176 |

Delivering Bad News in Good Ways:
Turn difficult conversations into purposeful dialogue, positive outcomes, & focused results in 3 easy steps

➤ What can we do to **get out of our own way** when faced with the need to deliver bad news?

➤ Is there a **process** for delivering bad news in good ways?

Now that you have finished this book you have more information to answer those questions. Let's continue the beach analogy.

There you are, treading water, caught in the undertow. You feel as though you're being carried out to sea. It is the hardest thing in the world to do, but THIS is the time to recognize that it is critical to slow down and craft your game plan.

While anyone else would start swimming frantically toward the shore, you take a virtual step back, collect information about your situation, and consider the options.

The advice in this book — if you internalize it, follow it, and practice it — gives you the confidence and knowledge to handle any challenging communication situation.

What would happen if you followed your first instinct and swam with all your might toward shore? That mighty undertow would work against you, and you would expend all your energy getting nowhere. You might even drown.

The first time you have to call upon the lessons in this book, you may feel a lot like the beach walker hit by a wave. Your brain may rebel against the advice to stop and think, because it is wired to do the opposite: react. As we know from previous chapters, nothing triggers your brain's instinct to react like fear (of pain, of rejection, of loss, of sadness, of anger).

One reaction is the instinct mentioned earlier, to try to swim like crazy toward shore. Another is to freeze — to do nothing. The reaction not to react is also fear-based.

We do not want to accept that we are in danger of drowning (talk about scary!), so we ignore the facts that are staring us right in the face. We are in water over our heads, being battered about by waves, and being towed out to sea by a force so powerful we are helpless to resist. One reaction is as dangerous as the other.

Delivering Bad News in Good Ways:
Turn difficult conversations into purposeful dialogue, positive outcomes, & focused results in 3 easy steps

| 177 |

Luckily for you, this book has helped you see that the instinct to procrastinate, to believe this situation will magically go away, can be overcome. Back to the analogy...

So there you are, treading water, when you notice that the undertow isn't moving you back, but sideways. You notice that when you stop struggling, you move parallel to the shoreline.

You wonder if, at some point, the force of the water will free you from its grasp and allow you to make for shore. You decide to try your theory and bob along for a bit. Then it happens. You feel the water's power relent. You swim to shore.

Your job is half over. You have battled with your own reaction to bad news (the monster wave), and now you must warn the other people walking along the shoreline.

As we have established, change to the current state is a challenge because we all have different tolerance thresholds. We also have built-in biases based on our individual experiences. This skews our perception and creates blind spots for our options and choices.

This plays into one of the reasons it is so hard for people to hear and work through bad news. We opt for the path of least resistance in an effort to avoid or resist change.

In our beach analogy, the people on the beach are experiencing a peaceful day that they do not want interrupted. This is not that different from stakeholders in our projects. They, too, enjoy when an environment is free of conflict. They do not want their peace interrupted.

Lucky for you, the second half of this book has given you the tools you will need. Using the **SED Method**, you can put your adventure in perspective before telling your story.

| 178 |

Delivering Bad News in Good Ways:
Turn difficult conversations into purposeful dialogue, positive outcomes, & focused results in 3 easy steps

- You will **separate** your own frightening experience from the danger at hand.

- You will **evaluate** the need to tell the people on the beach about this danger, the best ways to tell them, and the parts of the story that will best help them understand.

- You will **deliver** the information in an empathetic manner, you will give the facts before your opinion, and you will tell them the truth.

As time goes on, you will use the tools in this book to recognize bad news, deal with it, and share it when it is necessary. This advice will not eliminate your emotional reaction to bad news, but practice will help you to control it.

My wish for you is that each time you have to share bad news, the wave gets smaller until you barely get wet.

Delivering Bad News in Good Ways:
Turn difficult conversations into purposeful dialogue, positive outcomes, & focused results in 3 easy steps

| 179 |

ACKNOWLEDGMENTS

PROJECT TEAM

I want to kick off this section with celebrating the amazing team who pulled this project across the finish line.

Let's start with my dedicated, top shelf US-based editor Donna Capodelupo. A member of the 2003 Pulitzer Prize-winning Eagle-Tribune newsroom team, she is a freelance editor and a Communications Facilitator in the education field. Donna went above and beyond to clean up my writing and help ensure flow and consistency. The analogy in Chapter 9 was even born out of a dream she had about the material; now that's commitment! Thank you, Donna, for your flexibility, patience, and constant support. Learn more about Donna's talents at *donnacapodelupo@wordpress.com.*

I met Gurman deep Singh, my long time India-based graphic artist, when I was the Chief Digital Officer (CDO) for an outdoor shopping television show. Talented and always responsive, Gurman's work helped us push our brand deeper into the marketplace. Considerate, creative, and thorough, he never fails to deliver quality. Thank you, Gurman, for dedicated support and creativity over the years and for always providing a winning delivery. Please check out Gurman's creativity at *www.ddeskmultimedia.com.*

Diego Schtutman, an Argentina-based artist, provided the illustration for the book cover. He came to our team late in the game, but delivered quick, focused results. Before Diego came on the scene, we had several rounds of book cover reviews searching for the right visual to convey the voice and content of this book and for the entire series that will follow. We found his work, provided a creative brief, and he nailed it the first time with no revisions. Thank you, Diego, for your prompt response and powerful results. Check out more of Diego's work at *www.behance.net/curvabezier.*

FAMILY

I want to thank my husband, Ken Sigmon, and my two children Luda Sigmon and Ethan Sigmon for their patience, love, and support throughout this project, which actually began in late 2012. They tolerated skipped meals,

| 180 |

Delivering Bad News in Good Ways:
Turn difficult conversations into purposeful dialogue, positive outcomes, & focused results in 3 easy steps

missed phone calls, and long stretches of me going down the obsessed rabbit hole (as I tend to do!) for long periods when researching and writing this book and while working on other projects at the same time. Not sure how they put up with me but so glad they do!

I must thank my parents Phil Hadley, DDS and Elizabeth Hadley, MD who have never failed to be my number one fan throughout any hair-brained, time-suck project of mine. This ranged from them suffering through plays and musicals I wrote, produced, costumed, and acted in as a child to them being my first angel investors for a patent pending employee performance assessment and engagement software as a service (SaaS) concept that we designed and partially developed several years ago.

Ever patient with my busy-ness, they leave beautiful voice mails, send encouraging emails and text (I do read them!), and send loving cards even when I fail, at times, to give a timely response. P.S. I promise I'll call back soon (like you haven't heard THAT before)!

I must also thank my other parents, Bill and Nancy Walter, who unfortunately left this world years ago but have never left my heart. Their words, intelligence, and insights (and feistiness) were gifts that guide me daily. Intense debates, logic challenges, and test of wit were standard fare in our home when I was a child. I do miss them so. Thankfully, relationships never end; they simply change status.

Acknowledgment of my family support would not be complete without mentioning my aunt, Judy Maxwell, who also never fails to lend emotional and moral support as well as IT help! She's as tech savvy as any millennial hipster I've ever seen.

MENTOR

The stars must have been aligned the weekend when Jan Renerts Newton and I met at The Citadel Foundation Class Chairman Conference nearly two decades ago. From the moment we began chatting on that tour bus until the end of the weekend, I don't think we stopped talking. Then, a month later she sent me an email that simply said, "Coming to Charleston for the football game. Let's talk about working together." With that, on the 50-yard line of a The Citadel football game my life took an unexpected direction.

Delivering Bad News in Good Ways:
Turn difficult conversations into purposeful dialogue, positive outcomes, & focused results in 3 easy steps

| 181 |

To that point I was convinced I would spend my life as a therapist, but instead of helping one or a few people at a time, Jan opened the door to helping larger groups of people around the world. It was then that my mission to "help others help themselves" took on new meaning. Thank you, Jan, for your wisdom, experience, and generous love and objectivity.

WRITING SUPPORT

This book has been an on and off again project, but it really picked up steam when I joined the *Self-Publishing School (SPS)*. Chandler Bolt and his high performing team have a buttoned-down system for writing and publishing that I highly recommend to any aspiring or established writer.

With my membership to SPS, I was connected with two inspiring women who have walked with me through this process. Their unwavering support, enthusiastic energy, immense talent, and powerful presence put them in the same league as Sheryl Sandberg and the Lean In movement.

Thank you to my writing coach, Emily Rose, author of **Breaking Your Bad Love Habits,** for her insight, wisdom, and loving push to help me get out of my own way. Emily guided the entire process — structure, focus, cover art, sub-title, and publishing tips. I simply cannot thank you enough, Emily, for sharing your deep well of experience and knowledge and for your well-timed pushes when I lagged. Take a look at the impactful things Emily offers at her website *http://emilyrosecoaching.com/.*

I also must give a BIG thank you to my "book buddy" Kathryn Jones, author of **Automate Your Routines Guarantee Your Results**. We walked the publishing journey every week for more than three months. Wicked smart, creative, and super funny, before my eyes I watched her redefine what it is to market books in today's fast-paced, digital world. Kathryn is a young woman to watch. We'll see many more great things from her for a long time to come. Check out her work at *www.booksbykathryn.com.*

| 182 |

Delivering Bad News in Good Ways
Turn difficult conversations into purposeful dialogue, positive outcomes, & focused results in 3 easy steps

WRITING & DESIGN FEEDBACK & CONSTANT, UNWAVERING SUPPORT

THANK YOU, THANK YOU, THANK YOU, THANK YOU, THANK YOU!!!!!!! Words cannot express the gratitude I feel for some very special people who gave their time and energy to help me sort through content and design of this book — they read, discussed, and cheered throughout the process. So, here's a special thank you to them: Giselle Achecar, Clay Allison, Kevin Arends, Jennifer Zeppelin Berscheidt, Meredith Blair, Kimberly Brecko, Chris Davies, Bob Embleton, Adrienne Fritz, Olin Hyde, Andy Kaufman, Shannon Mease, Sam Morton, Jan Renerts Newton, Rich Rygg, Ben Snyder, and Cary Weber.

FINAL THANK YOU

To my awesome book Launch Team, Self-Publishing School Community, and all my friends in my giving, always responsive Facebook community. Your unselfish support, generous advice, and encouragement helped me through this process more than you will ever know. Thank you!

Delivering Bad News in Good Ways:
Turn difficult conversations into purposeful dialogue, positive outcomes, & focused results in 3 easy steps.

| 183 |

BIBLIOGRAPHY & CREDITS

INTRODUCTION

Schwartz, N. D. (2016, March 19). Carrier Workers See Costs, Not Benefits, of Global Trade. NY Times. Retrieved March 19, 2016, from *http://www.nytimes.com/2016/03/20/business/economy/carrier-workers-see-costs-not-benefits-of-global-trade.html*

CHAPTER 2

Soman, D. et al (2005). The Psychology of Intertemporal Discounting: Why are Distant Events Valued Differently from Proximal Ones? Retrieved April 2013 *http://faculty.som.yale.edu/ShaneFrederick/Marketing%20Letters.pdf*

CHAPTER 3

Hsu, C. (2012, February 22). Psychologists: Physical and Social Pain Hurts the Same Way. Retrieved March 11, 2012, from *http://www.medicaldaily.com/psychologists-physical-and-social-pain-hurts-same-way-239832*

Marks, D. (n.d.). The Fatal Flaw - The Most Essential Element for Bringing Characters to Life. Retrieved February 11, 2016, from *http://www.writersstore.com/the-fatal-flaw-the-most-essential-element-for-bringing-characters-to-life*

Thomas, K.W. (2012, June) What fear can teach us [Video file]. Retrieved from *https://www.ted.com/talks/karen_thompson_walker_what_fear_can_teach_us*

CHAPTER 4

Block, R. A., Handcock, P. A., & Zakay, D. (2010, April 18). How cognitive load affects duration judgments: A meta-analytic review. Retrieved November 29, 2012, from *http://peterhancock.cos.ucf.edu/wp-content/uploads/2012/06/Block-Hancock-Zakay-2010.pdf*

| 184 |

Delivering Bad News in Good Ways:
Turn difficult conversations into purposeful dialogue, positive outcomes, & focused results in 3 easy steps

Brooks, D. (2011). The social animal: The hidden sources of love, character, and achievement. New York: Random House. p 326.

Cron, L. (2012). Wired for story: The writer's guide to using brain science to hook readers from the very first sentence. New York: Ten Speed Press. p 7.

Fisher, R., Ury, W., & Patton, B. (1991). Getting to yes: Negotiating agreement without giving in. New York, NY: Penguin Books.

Holt, D. (2008, January 08). The Role of the Amygdala in Fear and Panic. Retrieved November 29, 2012, from http://serendip.brynmawr.edu/exchange/node/1749

Systemation. (2007). Maximizing Project Success Through People [Training Manual]. Colorado. www.systemation.com

CHAPTER 5

Blaber, P. (2008). The mission, the men, and me: Lessons from a former Delta Force commander. New York: Berkley Caliber.

Brizendine, L. (2006). The female brain. New York: Morgan Road Books. p 3.

Brooks, D. (2011). The social animal: The hidden sources of love, character, and achievement. New York: Random House.

Green, M. (2013). Visual Expert Human Factors: Errors in Eyewitness Identification Procedures. Retrieved April 13, 2013, from http://www.visualexpert.com/Resources/mistakenid.html

Neighmond, P. (2011, April 29). Think You're An Auditory Or Visual Learner? Scientists Say It's Unlikely. Retrieved April 116, 2012, from http://www.npr.org/sections/health-shots/2011/08/29/139973743/think-youre-an-auditory-or-visual-learner-scientists-say-its-unlikely

Nishizawa, S., Benkelfat, C., Young, S. N., Leyton, M., Mzengeza, S., Montigny, C. D., . . . Diksic, M. (1997, May 13). Differences between males and females in rates of serotonin synthesis in human brain. Retrieved April 16, 2012, from http://www.ncbi.nlm.nih.gov/pmc/articles/PMC24674/

Delivering Bad News in Good Ways:
Turn difficult conversations into purposeful dialogue, positive outcomes, & focused results in 3 easy steps

185

Quoidbach, J., Gilbert, D. T., & Wilson, T. D. (2013, January 24). The End of History Illusion. Retrieved March 08, 2013, from *http://science.sciencemag. org/content/339/6115/96 Science Vol. 339, Issue 6115, pp. 96-98*

CHAPTER 6

Tetlock, P., & Gardner, D. (2015). Superforecasting The Art and Science of Prediction. Crown.

How can you achieve new growth by discovering unexpected consumer insights? (n.d.). Retrieved March 04, 2016, from *http://www.innosight.com/ impact-stories/vf-lee-case-study.cfm*

CHAPTER 7

Baile, W. F., Buckman, R., Lenzi, R., Glober, G., Beale, E. A., & Kudelka, A. P. (n.d.). The Oncologist. Retrieved January 12, 2012, from *http://theoncologist. alphamedpress.org/content/5/4/302.full*

Brown, P. B. (2008, November 25). Finding the Best Ways to Break Bad News. Retrieved April 02, 2016, from *http://www.nytimes.com/2008/11/25/ business/smallbusiness/25toolkit.html*

Williams, G. A., & Miller, R. B. (2002, May). Change the Way You Persuade. Retrieved April 01, 2012, from *https://hbr.org/2002/05/change-the-way-you-persuade*

CHAPTER 8

Isaacs, W. (1999). Dialogue and the art of thinking together: A pioneering approach to communicating in business and in life. New York: Currency.

Ariely, D. (2012, October). Dan Ariely: What makes us feel good about our work? [Video file]. Retrieved from *https://www.ted.com/talks/dan_ariely_what_makes_us_feel_good_about_our_work*

ILLUSTRATIONS, AUTHOR IMAGE, & COVER

Cover Illustration. Diego Schtutman *www.behance.net/curvabezier*

Chapter Images. Diego Schtutman © *123RF.com*

Thinking Process Graphic & Book Jacket. Gurman deep Singh
www.ddeskmultimedia.com

Author photo courtesy of Sean Maguire

MANUSCRIPT PREP & DESIGN

Happy Self Publishing

Delivering Bad News in Good Ways:
Turn difficult conversations into purposeful dialogue, positive outcomes, & focused results in 3 easy steps

| 187 |

ABOUT THE AUTHOR

Alison Sigmon is a longtime PMP certified project manager, clinical therapist, and business executive. She has co-founded or worked with several startup companies in the digital space. Companies and organizations around the world have relied on her expertise to train, facilitate, consult with, and coach tens of thousands of people. She has won several awards for her leadership and training efforts.

She has led projects for the following: software and user experience design; digital content strategy; brand design and development; marketing, advertising, and communications strategy; business development and fundraising; video design and production; and ecommerce.

Her efforts focus on the behavioral side of project management and relationships. Articles, presentations, and training materials can be found at several noted digital and traditional publications and her website at www.alisonsigmon.com.

Delivering Bad News in Good Ways is Alison's first book, and the first in a series on the subject.

An avid distance runner, writer, hiker, and traveler, Alison is a Gulf War veteran.

| 188 |

Delivering Bad News in Good Ways:
Turn difficult conversations into purposeful dialogue, positive outcomes, & focused results in 3 easy steps

LET'S CONNECT!

I'd love to hear your thoughts, stories, and insights. Please reach out anytime at one of the following:

Website: *www.alisonsigmon.com*

Email: *alison@alisonsigmon.com*

LinkedIn: *http://www.linkedin.com/in/alisonsigmon*

Twitter: *@alisonsigmon*

Facebook: *https://www.facebook.com/asigmon*

Instagram: *https://www.instagram.com/ahsigmon/*

Pinterest: *https://www.pinterest.com/ahsigmon/*

Delivering Bad News in Good Ways:
Turn difficult conversations into purposeful dialogue, positive outcomes, & focused results in 3 easy steps

| 189 |

Made in the USA
Columbia, SC
27 October 2018